GUARDIANS
of
VIRTUE

GUARDIANS
of
VIRTUE

Salem Families in 1800

BERNARD FARBER

Basic Books, Inc., Publishers

New York   London

Library of Congress Catalog Card Number: 70-174812
SBN 465-02784-9
Manufactured in the United States of America

Preface

The Puritan family has received some attention in sociological and historical literature pertaining to the origins of American society. The aftermath of Puritanism, on the other hand, generally has been ignored, particularly by family sociologists. The tendency has been to focus rather upon the effects of urbanization and industrialization on family organization. In doing so, sociologists make the implicit assumption that the period immediately following the decline of Puritanism is of little theoretical significance.

This book suggests that the post-Puritan time period, about the time of the American Revolution, may provide some valuable insight into the relationship between religious ideas and subsequent social structures, especially the family and economic and political institutions. In particular, the study of the aftermath of Puritanism may produce data relevant to Max Weber's hypothesis regarding the influence of "the Protestant ethic" on "the spirit of capitalism." In addition, such an analysis of the post-Puritan society may fix guidelines for investigating ideological influences on family organization in contemporary society.

The study of the family in Salem, Massachusetts, would not have been possible but for the publications of the Essex Institute which cover the history of Essex County. This study relied heavily upon the *Essex Institute Historical Collections*, the diary of The Reverend William Bentley, and the *Salem Vital Records to 1840*—all publications of the Essex Institute. My debt to the Essex Institute is obvious.

Wherever possible, I retained the spelling, punctuation, grammar, and capitalization of the documents quoted. Changing these in some instances might have affected the quality of the communication.

Support for this study was provided by the Graduate Research Board of the University of Illinois, Urbana, and the Children's Research Center (Public Health Research Grant MH-07346 from the National Institute of Mental Health).

I am particularly grateful to Louis Schneider (University of Texas), Julian Simon (University of Illinois), and Socorro Carino (University of Illinois) for their valuable criticisms and comments on the manuscript. I value the assistance of Vance Ahlf, Michael Benson, Margaret Brown, Michael Farber, Joan Krikelas, and especially Miss Carino. I also appreciate the patience and exceptional secretarial skills of Mrs. Sharon Cook, and the resources provided by the University of Illinois Library. I would also like to thank my wife Rosanna for her forbearance and for her painstaking review of the last chapter. My greatest debt, however, is to my parents, to whom I dedicate this book.

Bernard Farber

Contents

x

*   *   *

Contents

Figures

Tables

GUARDIANS
of
VIRTUE

1

Puritanism, Family, and Capitalism

The Puritan family, expressing the religious ideals of New Englanders, is considered by social scientists to provide a basic model from which the modern American family developed. Historians specializing in the colonial era, like Edmund S. Morgan (1966), have contended, moreover, that the Puritans ascribed even more importance to their families than to their religion. "The Puritan system failed because the Puritans relied upon their children to provide the church with members and the state with citizens. . . . They had allowed their children to usurp a higher place than God in their affections" (Morgan, 1966, pp. 185-186).

Despite interest by historians in the colonial Puritan family, there has been little scholarly study of the family during the period between the Puritan village organization and the emergence of the Industrial Revolution. The implication of this neglect is that the Industrial Revolution had a direct influence upon the Puritan style of family life. Yet the period roughly between 1775 and 1825 marked a commercial era which represented neither the Puritan (farming or fishing) village nor industrial New England. Analysis of the social structure of Salem, Massachusetts, during those transitional years may provide some insight into the relationship between family life, religious ideas, demographic and technological changes, and the "spirit of capitalism" in an American context.

Puritan Village Families and Later Entrepreneurship

Several historical studies of seventeenth-century Puritan family life have been made recently (Morgan, 1966; Demos, 1970; Greven, 1966; Powell, 1963). Together, they depict family life in various Puritan settlements such as Sudbury and Plymouth, Massachusetts. The diversity of norms governing economic and political life among these settlements is immediately apparent. First, even within communities, founders were drawn from various sections of England where patterns of land settlement and government differed considerably. Second, the relative autonomy of these colonial communities produced many variations in the creation of governmental offices and in ways of handling disputes. The Massachusetts Body of Liberties in 1641 empowered each town to establish its own constitution and bylaws. There were, however, some important

* * *

similarities particularly pertaining to membership in a corporate community. This membership was generally connected with the church (or at least with conformity to
church prescriptions).

Puritan Households

In his description of Plymouth housing in the seventeenth century, Demos (1970, pp. 46-51) emphasizes the
crowded conditions under which families lived. During the
long, cold winter, large families would generally occupy a
single warm room; other rooms, such as upstairs bedrooms,
being closed off, would be devoid of heat. Privacy was an
unheard-of luxury, and Demos notes that, while interaction
among family members within the household might be
highly controlled and restrained, numerous open disagree-
ments between neighbors (frequently ending in court)
would arise. Inhibition of aggressive acts seems to have
been necessary to maintain peace within the household
(not to mention one's sanity), but the consequent tension
seems to have resulted in quarrels, spitefulness, and fights
with neighbors. This expression of tension may have
fostered strong community controls over deviant action.

Marriage resulted from the decision to enter into a
married status rather than from falling in love. Although
marriages were based mainly on personal rather than
parental choice, there is evidence of bargaining over
parental wedding gifts before banns were issued. Bargaining was especially significant in second marriages, in which
the widow or widower could use his spouse's estate to
strike a good marital bargain. After betrothal at least two
weeks elapsed before the couple was married. Upon marriage a couple would occupy its own domicile; marriage
thereby afforded an escape from the crowded parental

household. The high rate of remarriage may have also contributed to crowded housing conditions. Forty percent of men and 26 percent of women over 50 years of age had been married more than once (following widowhood); the subsequent marriages yielded additional children.

Male dominance in the marital relationship was evident in many ways. The man was legally the head of the household, holding the status of freeman with a right to vote. Whereas married or betrothed women's infidelity was considered as adultery, married men could indulge in sexual intercourse with single women without being labeled as adulterous. Yet severe limits were placed upon the male prerogative. A husband could not strike his wife, nor "could he command her to do anything contrary to the laws of God, laws which were explicitly defined in the civil code" (Morgan, 1966, p. 45). On the contrary, women held a superior family status to both their sons and daughters. Women could inherit property and enter into contracts. A widow frequently became executrix of her husband's estate.

Given the crowded households, parental authority in maintaining order among the children had to be firm. At any given point in time the average household held about three children (Demos, 1970, p. 68). Although children were probably given somewhat free rein during their early years, by the age of six or seven they were expected to behave like little adults. Somewhere between the ages of eight and fifteen, they were ordinarily placed outside the family in apprenticeships. However, the extent to which this was done is difficult to estimate.

In addition to children, households in seventeenth-century Puritan settlements generally contained servants (including laborers and apprentices) and elderly parents or

maiden aunts. About one-third of the families in Bristol,
Rhode Island, in 1689 had at least one servant in the household (Demos, 1970, p. 194). These household members
added to the crowded conditions and created additional
problems of authority and control. The home was the site
of a variety of activities—eating, sleeping, recreation,
"passing time," domestic manufacturing, birth, and death—
all under these crowded conditions.

Historians of the Puritan family agree generally with
regard to its characteristics. They differ mainly in their
explanations of the basis for the kind of family life led by
the Puritans. Some historians, like Demos (1970), place
more emphasis on material and economic conditions;
others, like Morgan (1966), give greater weight to the
Puritan ideology in molding family life. In any case, the
organization of the Salem family around 1800 cannot be
understood simply as an extension of Puritan households
in the seventeenth century. Only an investigation of what
occurred in the intervening years would suggest how material conditions and ideology interact to shape the characteristics of family life.

Economic Development

Family activities, as well as their religious, economic,
and political concomitants, changed as the village society
of seventeenth-century New England gave way to the commercial life of the eighteenth century. Just as housing
grew more elaborate and permitted greater privacy as time
went on, so did community life become more differentiated
with increasing economic specialization, with the institu-
tionalization of religious sects and denominations, and with
the emergence of the federal political system. Social structure enormously increased in its complexity during the

eighteenth century, and family life must have undergone a corresponding modification. As later chapters in this book suggest, by 1790 it was no longer appropriate to designate a single family form as *the* Plymouth family or *the* Salem family. Instead, family life differed significantly in various parts of the social structure.

Salem developed from a seventeenth-century fishing and agrarian village to a highly complex shipping-center by 1800. The industrial and commercial growth of Salem proceeded slowly during at least the first century of its existence. The latter part of the eighteenth century, however, produced a spurt in Salem's development. Between the census of 1754 and that of 1785, the population doubled: in 1754 there were 3,462 inhabitants, whereas the 1785 population was 6,923 (Phillips, 1937, p. 175; Bentley, 1905, I, p. 7). Then, in the brief span from 1785 to 1790, the population increased another 14 percent to 7,921 (Bentley, 1905, I, p. 212).

Early industry and commerce in seventeenth-century Salem was limited. Except for some illicit traffic, shipping was generally restricted to the necessities of life. In the late 1600s, the basic industries of Salem were fishing, shipbuilding, and trade. Fish was the major export commodity. Some of the vessels built in Salem were sold in Spain and England. Of the 26 vessels registered out of Salem in 1699, 17 had been built there (Phillips, 1937).

Industry in Salem during the 1720s and 1730s required little capital. Shipbuilding could be undertaken without considerable investment. "It did not require much of a plant. A sloping shore and a few sheds served all the necessary purposes" (Phillips, 1937, p. 121). In general, Salem was dominated by household industries. "Shoes were made in the little shoeshops and a considerable amount of cloth was woven. Under an act for the encour-

agement of cloth-making from native flax, John Thornton
of Salem won the prize in 1723 for the best linen presented" (Phillips, 1937, p. 121). While there was an
attempt to stimulate industry, there was no great surge of
industrialization. By the 1730s, the mode of commerce
began to change. "Formerly the English merchants sent
their goods to be sold on commission, but now the colonial merchants had capital to invest and they bought
English goods outright" (Phillips, 1937, p. 138).

By the 1760s, overseas trade expanded considerably.
There were more than 53 fishing boats and 35 trading vessels afloat in 1765 (Phillips, 1937, p. 239). Probably 60 or
70 persons in Salem owned at least a part interest in seagoing vessels. In the years 1750-1769, Salem may have produced 300-400 sea captains, and probably over 2,000
vessels had sailed in and out of the area. Main (1965, p. 38)
points out that "Salem's tax assessment roll for 1771 listed
thirty-six merchants and shipowners owning 200 pounds
worth of stock in trade, comprising one-eighth of the population."

The expansion of shipping was accompanied by a similar increase in shipbuilding and its related industries, as
well as in retailing and wholesaling. Manufacturing, however, remained in the hands of artisans and was closely
associated with the household.

Morison (1941, p. 30) emphasizes the upsurge in trade
toward the end of the eighteenth century. He writes: "On
Salem, in particular, the Revolution wrought an entire
change in commercial spirit. Before the war Salem was
mainly a fishing port. Privateering gave her seamen a
broader horizon and her merchants a splendid ambition."

The commercial life in Salem from 1790 to 1810 produced much optimism among the inhabitants. The Reverend William Bentley notes this optimism in his diary.

February 20, 1802: This trade of Ship Building & of Boat Build-
has been a profitable Trade in Salem. The increase of Trading
Shops is truely great. No Town of its population had so few 20
years ago & now the number is in the mouths of all the Inhabitants, & yet none have lost credit or failed.

In the years following the American Revolution, commerce intensified and expanded until the major part of the
population was largely absorbed in trade of one form or
another. Fuess (1956, p. 7) reports:

It was indeed an exciting time, a strange phase in the evolution
of the Puritan. The sailors, released from their home town inhi-
bitions, had thrilling adventures to relate, in which beauty and
desire inextricably blended. The range of Yankee thought and
experience was widened by their association with the ancient
and exotic Far East.

Salem reached its apex as a shipping center in the years
1807-1810 with a reported 41,000 tonnage of ships owned
there. This tonnage contrasts sharply with the 25,000 tons
reported in the years 1798-1800 and with the few hundred
tons reported in 1699 or the 88 ships owned in 1765 (Morison, 1941, p. 398, Appendix Table v).
However, since "the approach to Salem Harbor [was]
particularly difficult in thick weather or at night, on
account of the many islands and submerged rocks in the
bay," only small ships could be accommodated by the shal-
low harbor (Morison, 1941, p. 162). With the War of 1812
the number of merchant ships registered in Salem declined
from 182 in 1807 to 57 in 1815 (Morison, 1941, p. 217).
At that time many of the major merchants departed from
Salem for Boston and New York. Following the decline of
merchant shipping, funds that had been invested in over-

seas commerce were shifted to manufacturing and other forms of enterprise.

The shipping industry in Salem from 1790 to 1810 seems to represent "rational bourgeois capitalism." Obviously the worldwide trade in which the Salem merchants and their ships engaged involved much risk and speculation and brought large financial returns. Although there was an element of romantic adventure in the Salem shipping industry around 1800, especially in privateering, there were also various ethical standards and risk-reducing devices more consistent with rational bourgeois capitalism than with adventurist capitalism. These devices included (1) the establishment of insurance companies to cover cargo and ship losses, (2) the formation of a highly complicated network of partnerships so that losses in one partnership could be covered by gains in another, (3) the negative valuation and disdain of the slave trade by major shipowners and by the Salem èlite, and (4) the heavy reliance on credit in the financing of ships and voyages. In addition, shipping in some respects represented the use of a rationally organized productive unit in which the wage-earning mariners served as unbound labor for ship owners. By the nature of the industry, a ship on a voyage is isolated from family and home, and the bureaucratic authority on shipboard reflects a rational division of labor.

Throughout New England history, the government had encouraged manufacturing. "The general court was busy as early as 1640 in efforts to encourage the manufacture of linen and cotton. . . . In 1645 the legislature began to encourage the importation and breeding of sheep, for the increase of woolen fabrics, as well as the sowing of flax and hemp, and established a state agency for the purchase of cotton at Barbados" (Rantoul, 1897, p. 9). This encouragement, including government bounties, however, occurred within the context of scarce money, household industry, and Puritan dominance.

Industrialization did not occur in Essex County generally until after the Revolution and in Salem itself until the decline in shipping. Morison (1941, p. 224) reports that it was not until 1848, "with the establishment of the Naumkeag Steam Cotton Mills, [that] Salem entered the factory era." The first Essex County cotton mill was introduced in Beverly in 1788 (Rantoul, 1897, pp. 1-43). "In 1794 thirty citizens of Newburyport raised $300,000 for a Woolen Manufactory. This particular project failed, but Essex County was soon to find plenty of capital for the financing of similar plans" (Fuess, 1956, p. 9). The post-Revolutionary spurt in industrialization can be exemplified by Lynn (also in Essex County). It illustrates the constant accelerated movement in the industrial expansion toward the end of the eighteenth century. "Ladies' shoes had been made 'at a very early period' and their manufacture had long been 'the principal occupation of the inhabitants.' As early as 1651 the shoemakers of Lynn had become a corporation. Eighty-thousand pairs of shoes were made in 1767, and this output had increased by 1810 to one million pairs. By 1855, with the introduction of modern machinery, more than ten million pairs were being turned out annually" (Fuess, 1956, p. 9). The population of Lynn increased from 2,295 in 1790 and 2,837 in 1800 to 14,257 in 1850. Hence the expansion in industry and population seems to have come fairly rapidly in the early nineteenth century with the introduction of modern technology.

In summary, historical studies reveal a growing complexity of the social structure of Salem during the seventeenth and eighteenth centuries. Investigations of the

* * *

seventeenth-century Puritan family indicate a tendency for
(1) families to live in cramped quarters, (2) interaction
among family members to be highly controlled and
restrained, (3) marriage to be based primarily on personal
choice, (4) males to be dominant, (5) parental authority
to be firm, and (6) the home to be the focal point of both
productive and recreational activities. Demos ascribes these
tendencies to the material conditions under which the New
England Puritans lived; Morgan places greater emphasis on
the Puritan ideology. Regardless of the basis for these pro-
clivities, by the end of the eighteenth century, the material
conditions and the social structure of Salem had changed
considerably. The population increased manifold, Salem
became a major seaport and shipping center, and manufacturing in Essex County grew. These changes imply a highly
differentiated social structure. However, if the material
and socioeconomic conditions of the Salem inhabitants
changed so markedly during the seventeenth and eighteenth
centuries, the question remains: Did the characteristics of
family life depicted in the studies of the early New England
Puritan family persist despite all these changes? If so, then
we must assign greater weight to the Puritan family ideology
than to material conditions in interpreting the historical
material; if not, we must stress material and socioeconomic
conditions more.

Puritanism and Social Structure in Salem

In his history of *Salem in the Eighteenth Century*, James
Duncan Phillips (1937, pp. 443-452) attributes the nature
of the town's social life to its Puritan background. He
regards the seventeenth century as laying the "foundation
of religion which demanded a strict individual responsi-

bility of every person" and contends that there was only a gradual "subsidence of the doctrine of the Elect." Phillips believes that although the clergy retained its belief in predestination, there was a gradual shift to a belief that anyone who lived an upright and honorable life could achieve salvation. "It was too unreasonable to suppose that men were elected to salvation before they were born, and that nothing they could do would change their status." He suggests, however, that "this [decline in the doctrine of predestination] in no way relaxed the pressure on the individual. It held him up to a higher standard of conduct, if anything, than before."

Like Max Weber, Phillips places much emphasis upon religious factors in the daily lives of the New Englanders. "The social philosophy of Salem, like that of all New England, was based on the tenets of Benjamin Franklin, which in turn had their roots in the religious life of the people" (Phillips, 1937, p. 447).

The position taken by Bailyn (1955) in interpreting the relationship between religious belief and social structure is opposed to that of Phillips. In his analysis of early American enterprise, he proposes that during the seventeenth century "economically all-powerful, politically influential but circumscribed, the merchants—willingly or not—were prime movers in a gradual, subtle, but fundamental transformation of New England society. Their involvement in the world of Atlantic commerce committed them to interests and attitudes incompatible with life in the Bible Commonwealth. Most of them did not seek the destruction of the Puritan society; but they could not evade the fact that in many ways commercial success grew in inverse proportions to the social strength of Puritanism."

Bailyn (1955, p. 105) comments on the incompatibility between Puritanism and the needs of entrepreneurs for the

free movement of people and goods and for an expanding
population. He notes that these needs contradicted the
requirement of the Puritan community of isolation from
contamination by strangers who might not submit to
Puritan authority. The Bailyn position implies that the
restrictions on New England entrepreneurship by the
British actually prolonged the lifespan of Puritan institutions.

The contradictory interpretations by Phillips and
Bailyn of the effect of Puritanism on the later development of New England social structure echo the explanations by Demos and Morgan regarding Puritan family life.
Together, they indicate that both religious and economic
factors are important for understanding the Salem family
of 1800. Max Weber's analysis of the implications of Puritanism for historical process and Philippe Ariès's views of
the effects of the shift from apprenticeships to schooling
in training people seem particularly relevant—Weber for
introducing religious factors and Ariès for economic
influences.

Max Weber and Religion

Although Max Weber did not write extensively about the
family as such, his views on the effects of Puritanism on
social structure are highly relevant to the study of the
family. He gave the concept of "calling" a central position
in his analysis of Puritanism as religious doctrine and the
spirit of capitalism. A secular calling is the fulfillment of
man's duty to God in worldly affairs. Accordingly, the secular calling is a singular life-task devoted to God. The Puritans upheld their principle of ascetic conduct, at least
ideally, in all areas of life and avoided "the spontaneous

enjoyment of life and all it had to offer" (1958, p. 166).
Accordingly, they deprecated such nonrational aspects of
life as sports or theater, which they considered an irrational
use of time and wealth. Weber indicates that "the religious
valuation of restless, continuous, systematic work in a
worldly calling, as the highest means to asceticism, and at
the same time the surest and most evident proof of rebirth
and genuine faith, must have been the most powerful con-
ceivable lever for the expansion of that attitude toward life
which we have here called the spirit of capitalism" (1958,
p. 172). Secular callings extended to all facets of life, including the family.

Weber finds the basis for the calling a means for
maintaining a relationship between man and God in the
Calvinist doctrine of predestination. "By founding its
ethic in the doctrine of predestination, it [Calvinism]
substituted for the spiritual aristocracy of Monks outside
of and above the world a spiritual aristocracy of the predestined saints of God within the world" (1958, p. 121). The
success and usefulness of one's work is the "means of know-
ing one's state of grace . . . [when these works] are performed solely for the glory of God" (1958, p. 141). Business
success could then be equated with the success of the calling, and individuals and their fellow men could be apprised
of their state of grace. A community of the elect could thus
be identified. Certainty in their membership among the
elect, according to Weber, marks "those self-confident
saints whom we can rediscover in the hard Puritan merchants of the heroic age of capitalism" (1958, p. 112).
Weber considers the close relationship between predestination and calling as the core of the Puritan ethic, which he
regards as the purest form of Protestantism, providing a
basis for the spirit of capitalism.

* * *

Puritanism, Family, and Capitalism

Although Puritans obviously did not invent capitalism, their conception of secular calling may have elevated this instrumental, practical institution into an ethical imperative. In doing so, according to Weber's conception, men ideally devoted their energies and time to this task. This devotion in turn was rewarded financially as an indication of success and, by implication, predestined election. By taking their secular calling seriously, the Puritans refined the precepts and practices of capitalism.

The ultimate significance of Puritanism for Weber lay in the scheme of rewards and punishments it applied in guiding the conduct of its adherents. To provide sanctions in a code of conduct, Puritanism (like any other ideology) had to be translated into prescriptions governing the basic institutions of the society. According to Weber:

> . . . It is not the ethical *doctrine* of a religion, but that form of ethical conduct upon which *premiums* are placed that matters. Such premiums operate through the form and the condition of the respective goods of salvation. And such conduct constitutes "one's" specific "ethos" in the sociological sense of the word. For Puritanism, that conduct was a certain methodical, rational way of life which—given certain conditions—paved the way for the "spirit" of modern capitalism. The premiums were placed upon "proving" oneself before God in the sense of attaining salvation—which is found in *all* Puritan denominations—and "proving" oneself before men in the sense of socially holding one's own within the Puritan sects. Both aspects were mutually supplementary and operated in the same direction; they helped to deliver the "spirit" of modern capitalism, its specific *ethos*: the ethos of the modern *bourgeois middle classes*. [Gerth and Mills, 1946, p. 321]

The idea of a Covenant of Grace dominated New England colonial society (Miller, 1949). From their first voyage to America, the New England Puritans thought of themselves as the analog of the early Israelites who had made a pact with God. The Puritans added to the doctrinal positions of Luther and Calvin the idea of their role as a chosen people destined to form a society based on the obligation to righteousness. They regarded their role in history as being a demonstration to England and Europe of the fulfillment of a divinely ordained society. Thus the towns of Massachusetts and Connecticut were not designed to be merely places of prosperity and contentment but were intended to be the heralds of a new social order. This concept of a communal covenant developed throughout the seventeenth century.

Weber and others stress that the Puritans, among whom the "spirit of capitalism" supposedly attained its epitome, modeled their family and kinship organization after the Jews of the Bible. Although the prevalence of Puritanism and Calvinism was considerably diminished prior to the flourishing of capitalism, the biblical form of family and kinship organization retained great vitality throughout the nineteenth century among the bourgeoisie. This family and kinship organization can be contrasted with the proletarian models and the Catholic prescriptions in Europe and America.

Among the chief characteristics ascribed by Weber to the Puritan saints is asceticism: the delay of immediate gratification and the repression of nonmarital eroticism. Taking the commandments of the Bible seriously, the Puritans suggested a similar strong asceticism among the ancient Hebrews. First, the emphasis on law in the Old Testament is suggestive of the importance given to strong conscience and self-control. These attributes can be viewed as a reaction to the hostility of the social and physical environment of the Hebraic tribes. The Ten Commandments and the rules for daily existence seemed necessary to inhibit conflict which might disintegrate the group. Second, the authority given to the patriarchs (modeled after God the lawgiver) would facilitate delayed-gratification patterns—given the stress on law. Third, the content of the Ten Commandments and other norms indicates the significance attached to sexual repression. Together, these conditions suggest a situation comparable to the Oedipal drama in psychoanalytic literature.

Although the doctrine of predestination may have been important in stimulating the conception of the "community of the elect," by the time capitalism emerged as a strong force in America after the Revolution, this doctrine was no longer held. What remained were institutional models that the Puritans patterned after those of the Israelites. Perhaps the most significant of these models is that of the biblical norms and values pertaining to family and kinship. The biblical form of family and kinship survived in the decline of Puritanism, and its remnants are still found in middle-class families and in the legal systems of New England states.

The Puritan use of the family to regulate the political, religious, and economic activities of its members created close, systematic interconnections among church, commerce, and government. A change in any of these spheres of activity would have strong repercussions in the others. The adaptations in the other spheres would then in turn affect the sphere in which modification was first observed. Because of the central role of the family in the lives of its members, it putatively became the clearinghouse through which revisions in other institutions were mediated. Although the family may not have provided an initial force in structuring other institutions, in the long run, its mediating role may have given it a major part in determining the course of community life. Possibly the familial epi-phenomenon of Puritanism and Calvinism is more respon-sible than particular religious beliefs in providing an impetus for the development of the spirit of capitalism.

If Max Weber is right, and if the family in Salem after the American Revolution represented a long-term expres-sion of Puritanism, then it would have to be organized in a way that would stimulate the development of modern, rational capitalism. Consequently, to the extent that Weber's ideas are relevant, the analysis will suggest how family attri-butes derived from the Puritan-based model affected eco-nomic development. Although social scientists disagree over Weber's precise interpretation of the characteristics of modern capitalism, the description presented below pro-vides a rough indication of his views (see Schneider, 1970).

Weber differentiated between capitalistic enterprise and the spirit of capitalism. He regarded capitalistic enterprise as existing throughout history. "Capitalism and capitalistic enterprises, even with a considerable rationalization of capi-talistic calculation, have existed in all civilized countries of the earth. . . . in China, India, Babylon, Egypt, Mediter-ranean antiquity, and the Middle Ages, as well as in modern times. These were not merely isolated ventures, but eco-nomic enterprises which were entirely dependent on the continual renewal of capitalistic undertakings, and even continuous operations" (1958, p. 19). Weber saw modern capitalism derived from the "spirit of capitalism" as a unique configuration of cultural elements. At various times, these elements have appeared separately in other cultures. Weber considered the construction of this particular configuration as the work of modern Protestant religious beliefs. Modern capitalism, according to him, consists of the following:

Maximization of Profits. Ideally, all other considera-tions are to be ignored. Family connections, traditional

norms and values, and personal friendships are subordinate
to profit. This implies that entrepreneurship is a religious-
like calling and is consistent with the Puritan doctrine that
man's relationship with God has priority over any ties with
man (see Marx, 1964, p. 35).

*"Rational Capitalistic Organization of [Formally] Free
Labor"* (1958, p. 21). Labor, as well as the products of capitalism, is a commodity which can be computed in terms of
profit and loss. Unlike the retention of apprentices, inden-
tured servants, or slaves, the services of free labor can be purchased only when required, and overhead is minimized. Moreover, with a free labor market, there is less opportunity for
the development of strong sentimental attachments (as well
as hatreds) which interfere with the rational and efficient
operation of the enterprise. There can be a surplus population of free laborers to maximize production efficiency
while minimizing costs. In contrast, the creation of perma-
nent obligations to a bound labor force inhibits turnover
when there are inefficient operations. The concept of free
labor as a commodity, like maximization of profits, is consistent with the subordination of relationships between
men to that between man and his God.

Separation of Business from Household. Consistent
with the emphasis upon free labor, the isolation of business
life from household affairs is seen by Weber as an important
characteristic of the modern capitalistic system. This separation defines the business economy as productive and the
household economy as consumptive. The consumptive
aspects of the household concern mainly the way of life
followed by family members. The separation of business
and household therefore involves the isolation of capitalistic enterprise from the style of life of those involved in
this enterprise. The attainment of wealth is separated from
spending or consumption patterns; an ascetic home life may

be coupled with the accumulation of capital; home government is independent of the management of enterprise. More obviously, the separation creates a network of business relationships outside of the family. These business ties can then be maintained on a rational, competitive basis, whereas family ties and those concerned with household government necessarily involved nonrational norms and obligations.

Rational Bookkeeping. The elimination of personal ties and the other nonrational elements from business enterprise implies that all costs and income can be accounted for by efficient bookkeeping procedures. The development of rational accounting systems makes it possible to evaluate manufacturing costs, marketing, and prices, and to revise production procedures to maximize profits. In the long run, rational bookkeeping procedures can provide an objective standard for determining the degree of success in one's calling. Without such systematic bookkeeping it would be difficult to take advantage of the effects of free labor and to eliminate nonrational elements in maximizing profits.

In the analysis of data on Salem in 1800, special attention will be given to the extent to which a free labor market is encouraged as well as to the separation of business and households. These two areas of concern seem to pertain more to social structure than does the role of maximizing profits (as an end) and rational bookkeeping (as a means) in modern capitalism.

Philippe Ariès and the Economy

An alternative perspective for interpreting the relationship between family and society is taken by Philippe Ariès in his book *Centuries of Childhood* (1962). Although Ariès

does not attempt to show a precise relationship between
the family and the economy, his analysis implies a decline
of the economy based on medieval principles and a rise of
the economy with the characteristics attributed by Weber
to modern capitalism.

Philippe Ariès has suggested how the modern conjugal
family emerged out of the medieval social structure in
Europe. Relying upon the arts of the Middle Ages and the
Renaissance as well as the usual historical records (e.g., diaries, school records, personal accounts, official papers),
Ariès provides an imaginative account of the differentiation
which occurred over the centuries. He gives particular attention to ideas of (1) dependency in superordinate-subordi-
nate relationships and (2) the use of common space. Ariès
suggests that when differentiated social units (or persons
with different roles) occupy a common space, they develop
conceptions of rank or hierarchy in order to distinguish
superior from dependent members. In medieval Europe,
particularly France, this hierarchical arrangement was
ascribed through lineages or "houses." Lineages of peasants
were dependent upon nobles, and so on. Hence, the major
distinctions in rank were based on kinship ties. Since people
succeeded to the same occupational level as their parents,
kinship was an effective indicator of degree of dependency
in this situation. In distinguishing between social ranks, kinship was a more useful criterion than some other means,
such as age-grading; on this basis a noble child was superior
in rank to an elderly peasant. Thus, clear demarcations of
rank by kin group characterized medieval social structure.

As an historical demographer, Philippe Ariès places
much emphasis also on the decline in the risk of deaths of
very young children. He implies that during the Middle
Ages, the death rate for the very young was high, and there-

fore parents could not risk the investment of much capital
in the educational process. The apprenticeship system
afforded a means for socialization without such risk. As
hygienic conditions improved, the risk of losing children
declined, and parents now regarded it as worthwhile to
invest in their children. This investment included both emotional and financial resources.

Change in the educational institutions from the Middle
Ages to the modern era is, for Ariès, the event which initi-
ated the development of the modern conception of the
family. According to Ariès, in the Middle Ages educational
institutions were cloistered activities related directly to the
Church. They were meant primarily for clerics. The business of learning whatever skills were necessary for carrying
on an occupation was taken up through apprenticeship. In
apprenticeship, reading or writing or other necessary skills
were learned on the job. Consequently there was no age-
differentiation in educational institutions. However,
as these institutions became important for secular purposes, a wider range of lineal-descent groups was represented
in educational institutions. Children not only of the wealthy
and noble, but also of the poor and middle classes, began to
attend educational institutions as a form of preparation for
later life. Even in Catholic countries like France, upward
social mobility through the attainment of professional skills
became important. In the process, age-grading assumed a
significant social dimension. The age ranges of students
became more specialized at different levels of educational
institutions. Schools became more and more the province
of the young.

The decline of apprenticeship and rise of student classes,
from the Ariès viewpoint, was a significant one. As apprentices, the young were dependent upon their master not only
for proper socialization and learning skills, but also for food,

a place to sleep, and a place to live. The contract was
between the apprentice and his master. With the growth of
educational institutions, the contractual arrangement
changed. The primary parties to the contract were no
longer the student and the teacher, but the parents and the
teacher. The student relied on his parents for tuition and
the funds of board and room. The teacher now required
strong privileges for disciplining children (even corporal
punishment) because students were not directly dependent
upon him. The dependency of the young was thus no
longer directly tied to a lineal-descent group but rather to
the parent-child relationship. Instead of turning children
over to masters in apprenticeships, parents were now
responsible for their own children, and it became natural
for "families" to be defined in terms of these parent-child
units. Different lineages no longer tended to occupy a common space. The household consisting of parents and their
children became the basis for organizing family life. In the
process, the concept of "the family" as a conjugal unit with
strong emotional ties emerged.

The analysis by Ariès is relevant for the study of the
family in Salem in 1800 for several reasons. First, Salem
relied heavily upon the apprenticeship system, extending
these contracts to girls as well as boys. Apprenticeships
were lengthy, sometimes ranging over fifteen years. Second,
schools were founded early in Salem's history. At first these
were private schools which afforded a classical education.
By 1712, however, there was a public school system, and
children of all socioeconomic levels attended by the beginning of the nineteenth century (although only a minority
of the school-age children of Salem were students). Third,
with Salem's rapid growth as a seaport after the Revolution
(and its later decline), mortality rates fluctuated considerably. These rates affected family composition and depen-

dency relationships. Thus, the viewpoint of Ariès that
demographic, technical, and economic relationships were
the primary factors in defining family organization was
also taken into account in the analysis of the Salem family:
Who was in control over the lives of children—parents or
community?

Interaction Effects: Cultural Models and Material Conditions

The positions taken by Weber and by Ariès represent opposing views in historical explanation. The Weber approach is
that general norms and values in a society constrain people
to organize their everyday lives in certain ways. These
values provide molds for cultural models. His perspective
is that Puritanism provided the primary cultural models for
both family and economy. On the other hand, Ariès bases
his interpretation of history upon economic and property
relationships. As the control over children in the economy
shifted from nonfamilial functionaries(e.g., nobles, masters,
officials) to the parents, adjustments in guardianship had
to be made, and the conjugal family crystallized as a social
unit. Since Ariès drew most of his information from Catholic populations, he could not attribute this development of
the nuclear family as a social form to Puritanism or Calvinism. Although the religious foundations of his populations
had not changed, the locus of control over the occupational destinies of children had shifted, and Ariès perceived
this shift as the driving force in revising family organization.

    Here, then, are two alternative explanations of family
organization. Although they provide conflicting interpretations of the relationship between family and social structure, they are not necessarily mutually exclusive, but may

interact in a dialectical way. The Weber interpretation is
based upon cultural models which are (or have been)
explicit in religious ideologies. The Ariès interpretation
draws its significance from the proprietorship of the economic destinies of children.

This study of Salem families can then view the interaction of the biblical cultural model and the economic use of
children as distinct influences in shaping post-Puritan, pre-
industrial family organization. This analysis should help us
to understand how the family prepared for the later Industrial Revolution.

Conclusion: Family Guardianship, Succession, and Marital Alliances

In brief, Salem, Massachusetts, of 1800 represents a community which was strongly Puritan in history and largely
homogeneous ethnically. Inasmuch as it was founded and
dominated by Puritans, it was relatively uncontaminated
by other traditions, and a progression can be observed in its
transition from a Puritan community to a city, in many
ways embodying "the spirit of capitalism" by the beginning
of the nineteenth century. Although other influences, such
as the American Revolution, intrude, the Salem family can
be analyzed partly from the perspectives of Weber and Ariès.

The family was pervasive in Puritan and post-Puritan
society, acting like glue or connective tissue to bind religious and economic life together. First, the family served
as guardian over all areas of deportment and was particularly responsible for its members' spiritual and economic
well-being. Second, the transmission of both the state of
grace and economic welfare from one generation to the
next—the succession of divine and secular estates—was in

the family domain. Third, because guardianship and the inheritance of divine and secular estates varied by social status, marital alliances between families of the same class crystallized differences in religious belief and economic activities by socioeconomic level. Fourth, since the family was responsible for the socialization of children, the manner by which it inculcated ideas regarding religion and economy ensured the perpetuation of many Puritan standards of conduct. Consequently, although Puritanism disappeared by the time of the American Revolution, the Puritan-derived norms in family, economy, and politics remained. The analysis in this book is concerned with the interrelationships of the familial, economic, and political life of Salem.

In particular, this book pursues two lines of investigation: (1) that the adoption of the Biblical Judaic model of family organization by the Puritans helped to produce certain institutional norms which persisted long after Puritanism died away and which affected the economy indirectly, and (2) that as technological and demographic conditions changed, the family required various adaptations, and these adaptations were consistent with the development of industrial capitalism. The succeeding chapters are concerned with ways in which (a) family guardianship, (b) rules of succession, (c) creation of marital alliances, and (d) socialization of children in the Salem of the post-Revolutionary War period were associated with economic and political relationships.

2

The Puritan Ideology of Family Government

This chapter presents the ideological basis of the relationship between the economy, politics, and the family in
Salem to be discussed in succeeding chapters. In each
society, as children are socialized, arrangements must be
made for their guardianship. In Salem the family played a
major role in this guardianship. This chapter, relying in part
upon religious writings, first describes the Puritan family as
guardian. Second, it examines the decline of family guardianship in post-Puritan society. Third, it turns to socioeconomic variations related to family government and focuses
on the precarious situation of the lower-class family.
Finally, it deals with the problems in family guardianship,
particularly those created by illegitimacy and by the incapacitation of parents.

Puritan Family as Guardian

Max Weber wrote of the isolation of the Puritan from his fellow man deriving from the close relationship between a man and his God. Since human relationships were considered secondary, a man could justifiably exploit others in his attempt to demonstrate his predestined grace. Probably because of this emphasis, Weber paid little attention to the family in his discussion of the association between the Protestant ethic and the spirit of capitalism.

In his historical analysis of the Puritan family, Edmund Morgan (1966) placed the family at the center of Puritan ideology. This emphasis, according to Morgan, follows from the Puritans' attempt to model their lives after the norms of the ancient Hebrews. For the Puritans, the original Hebrew covenant included not only Abraham but his "seed" as well. The seed was interpreted to include not only his descendants—children, grandchildren, great-grandchildren, and so on—but also the other members of his household (such as servants or relatives). The Puritans, in reviving the Hebrew covenant, also undertook to fulfill the same obligations. This undertaking is evidence in statements such as those made by John Cotton: "If God make a Covenant, to be a God to thee and thine, . . . then it is thy part to see it, that thy children and servants be Gods people." In another context, Cotton extends this obligation: "When we undertake to be obedient to him [God, we undertake not only] in our owne names, for our owne parts, but in the behalfe of every soule that belongs to us . . . for our wives, and children, and servants, and kindred, and acquaintance, and all that are under our reach, either by way of subordination, or coordination" (cited in Morgan, 1966, p. 7).

The Puritan Ideology of Family Government

The Puritan conception of history was that the Jews had deviated from the norms which were derived from the covenant and thereby had lost their "chosen" status. The Puritans saw themselves as predestined to carry out the conditions of the covenant, and they took seriously the concept of authority. If God is the supreme authority, and the Puritans represent his elect, then it is reasonable that they should claim authority over the nonelect. According to Morgan, "The Puritans were no levelers. Social classes and the various offices, orders, and positions of social rank existed for them as part of a divinely ordered plan, 'so that it appears, [according to William Hubbard] whoever is for a parity in any Society, will in the issue reduce things into a heap of confusion'" (Morgan, 1966, p. 18).

Given this conception of the family and society, the major task of civil government was to oversee family heads in the performance of their duty. The Puritan leaders had no intention of making men "yield up their Family-Government over their Wives, Children, and Servants, respectively, to rule them in common with other Masters of Families" (Davenport, cited in Morgan, 1966, pp. 142-143). They were cognizant of the fact that without the assistance of household heads, they would be unsuccessful in accomplishing their task of establishing a saintly community. According to Morgan (1966, pp. 143-144):

The Puritans recognized this fact in characterizing families as "the root whence church and Commonwealth Cometh" (Boston Sermons, January 14, 1671-1672), "the Seminaries of Church and Commonwealth" (Eleazar Mather, *A Serious Exhortation*, p. 20), "the foundation of all societies" (Samuel Hooker, *Righteousness Rained from Heaven*, 1677, p. 25), and "the Nurseries of All Societies" (Cotton Mather, *A Family Well-Ordered*, 1699, p. 3). "*Well-ordered Families*," Cotton Mather explained, "naturally produce a *Good Order* in other *Societies*.

*   *   *

Guardians of Virtue

> When *Families* are under an *Ill Discipline*, all other *Societies*
> being therefore *Ill Disciplined*, will feel that Error in the *First*
> Concoction" (loc. cit.). "Such families are," James Fitch
> warned, "such at last the Church and Common-wealth must
> be" (*An Explanation of the Solemn Advice*, 1683, p. 15). If
> these statements were platitudinous, they nevertheless expressed
> the assumption upon which Puritan leaders acted, namely that
> the state is made up of families rather than individuals.

From the beginning efforts were made to place within a household every member of the community who was not a family head. Massachusetts in 1638 required each town to "dispose of all single persons and inmates within their towne to servise, or otherwise" (Morgan, 1966, p. 145).

The Puritans placed deviants, both adults and children, in the households of respectable family heads. Morgan suggests that "the punishment of sin in New England was aimed not so much at improving the sinners as it was at demonstrating to God that the ruler did not condone sin" (Morgan, 1966, p. 173).

There is a widespread impression that the Puritans in New England lived in an ascetic, humorless existence, with no finery and very little sex. This impression is consistent with the emphasis on thrift, diligent use of time, and dedication to one's secular calling, as prescribed in the writings of Benjamin Franklin (regarded by Max Weber as the epitome of the Puritan ethic).

Probably a more adequate representation of the Puritan perspective is the conception of good and evil as the opposition between the "natural" and the "unnatural" or "artificial." Whatever occurred in the natural order of things was good. Family government was based on natural relationships; hence, it was good. Social-status differentiation was also based on natural order, being derived from God, and was therefore to be sustained. Sex and God were natural, too, and not to be denied.

The naturalness of differences in social status was reflected in Puritan views on clothing. In 1651 the General Court ruled:

> Intollerable excesse and bravery hath crept in upon us, and especially amongst people of meane condition, to the dishonor of God, the scandall of its professors, the consumption of estates, and altogether unsuteable to our provertie. . . . [The Court declared its] utter detestation and dislike that men or women of mean condition, educations and callings should take upon them the garb of gentlemen by wearing of gold and silver lace, or buttons, or poynts at their knees, to walke in greate boots, or women of the same ranke to wear silke or tiffany hoodes or scarfes, which though allowable to persons of greater estate or more liberal education, yet we cannot but judge intollerable in persons of such like condition. [Waters, 1897, pp. 75-65]

Accordingly, in the mid-seventeenth century only persons with an estate of over 200 pounds, individuals "whose education or employments were above the ordinary," magistrates and their families, and military personnel, were exempted from fines for wearing finery. Thus, the Puritans used clothing as an outward sign of election.

The use of repressive sanctions, by which the Puritans have often been characterized, refers to their treatment of the "unnatural." This emphasis on the "natural" versus the "unnatural" can be observed in grounds for subjecting persons to the jurisdiction of families other than their own:

> Adults were also subjected to family government following the 1660's. One Abigail Roberts, for example, was presented [to the Court] from dressing in clothing finer than her station in life warranted and for living outside of family govern-

ment. . . . A more serious charge, against a widow having a child three years after her husband's death, resulted in her being whipped ten stripes and ordered "into some good family where shee may be under government." Charges of idleness, drunkenness, "idle reports to amuse the people," playing cards and keeping bad company, stubborn and wicked notions, and the wearing of men's clothes by a girl, thus "seeming to confound the course of nature," all resulted in persons being placed in family jurisdiction. [Towner, 1966, p. 422]

Families were advised by Cotton Mather not to hire "ungodly servants lest their children be corrupted by contagion," and above all marriages with the ungodly were to be avoided. Increase Mather warned that such marriages would cut off the offspring and their descendants from God's grace:

Take heed how you dispose of your Children. . . . It may make us dread to think what's coming, in that it is with us as it was with the old World, the Sons of God are marrying with the Daughters of men, Church Members in disposing of their Children look more at Portion than at Piety. . . . a sad sign that Religion will expire, and such Families be cut off from the Covenant, within a few Generations, and the branches thereof perish for ever. [cited in Morgan, 1966, pp. 181-182]

The divinely ordained status-ascription of children is apparent in Puritan writings. This doctrine is inherent in the belief that good can stem only from good and not from evil. The idea was sometimes stated as: "God casts the line of election in the loins of godly parents." This phrase ran through the writings of such men as Increase Mather:

Now God hath seen meet to cast the line of Election so, as that it doth . . . for the most part run through the loyns of godly parents . . . And there are some Families that the Lord hath Chosen above others and therefore poureth his Spirit upon the Offspring in such Families successively. [cited in Morgan, 1966, pp. 182-183]

*   *   *

Increase Mather was explicit in the claim that election was a divinely ascribed status. "Tho it be not wholly and only so, that Elect Parents have none but elect Children, or that elect children are alwaies born of elect Parents yet God hath seen meet to cast the line of election so, as that generally elect Children are cast upon elect Parents" (cited in Morgan, 1966, pp. 183-184). Other writers, such as Cotton Mather, Eleazar Mather, and Thomas Thatcher, made similar statements.

Because of the inheritance of the elect status, parents felt a strong obligation to exert their authority in matters of their children's occupation, marriage, and general deportment. The failure of the children to be successful in their lives was interpreted as a sign that the family really was not among the elect. Patriarchal family life, modeled after the ancient Jews, thus became an integral part of the Puritan social structure.

Post-Puritan Family and Community Guardianship

The ideology of family government is related to the Puritans' view of community. The conception of the community among the Puritans implied special privileges—as well as special responsibilities—for persons designated as members. Not all individuals living in a community like Salem were regarded by the Puritans as "inhabitants." The term "inhabitants" was "used to describe those who had been regularly propounded to the town and received or acknowledged as inhabitants. This left a number of residents not entitled to share in the common lands, many if not most of whom are included in the total enumeration [of the population of Salem in 1637] . . . as members of the families of 'inhabitants'" (Putnam, 1921, p. 149).

* * *

In estimating the population of Salem in 1637, Eben
Putnam (1921, pp. 149-150), reports difficulties in enumeration because of the residence of noninhabitants:

> Probable instances are Robert Gutch (Gooch), who was
> admitted as an inhabitant 23-10-1638, and had a grant of
> land 1-11-1637, but who was one of Richard Hollingworth's
> workmen, and prior to February, 1638, had married his
> master's daughter; and William Walker, who was in debt to
> Townsend Bishop, March 1637, and was probably a member
> of the latter's family in the following December. But there
> were several others whose names appear as having been
> admitted inhabitants and who evidently were in Salem in
> 1637, and yet who are not named in the list. In some cases
> they had evidently left town at the time the list was actually
> drawn up, which may not have been until the following
> spring. . . . for on 25-4-1638, it is stipulated that Richard
> Adams, Samuel Cornish, Widow Smith, and Grafton's
> mother-in-law, "forgotten," are to receive "their half acre
> apeece of marsh land."

The designation of inhabitant is related to the Puritan
doctrine of the elect and was initially applied to those persons predestined to achieve salvation. Undoubtedly, some
of the residents who were not inhabitants included tran-
sients, "persons as yet undecided where to settle, and who
would today be included in any census, and also there
would be a greater or less number of strangers, fishermen,
sailors, etc., whose stay would be brief, but who would add
materially to the transient population of the town proper"—
perhaps 100 persons in 1637 (Putnam, 1921, p. 150). More
significant was the group of families intending to become
inhabitants. "In most cases it was customary to delay admis-
sions for a sufficient time after the request had been made,
to discover any objection" (Putnam, 1921, p. 150). In this

*   *   *

The Puritan Ideology of Family Government

manner, "the community" remained an exclusively Puritan corporate body.

The seventeenth-century Puritans utilized the household to maintain control over deviants and noninhabitant residents. In particular, they used apprenticeships in attempting to control the style of life of the nonelect. The apprenticeship system provided a form of exchange whereby the deviant or the poor were inculcated with the norms and values of the Puritan way of life, while their masters obtained cheap labor. In essence, the nonelect were socially children and not "inhabitants":

> It was not merely those in need of alms who were subject to having their children taken away from them in what might be called legislation for the poor. Parents or masters who failed to raise their children or servants in a properly religious atmosphere, who neglected their instruction in reading, who failed to teach them the catechism, or who were not bringing them up to a secular calling, were equally likely to lose their wards to some other master. Single individuals of whatever age were required by law to place themselves under good family government, and even a few married persons—those whose family government failed—were placed under the jurisdiction of other families. The idle as well as the indigent; the loose liver as well as the lame, the halt, and the blind; the profligate as well as the poor orphan were trapped in the fine-mesh net of legislation for the poor. [Towner, 1966, p. 420]

As Puritanism declined, "secular poverty" more than "spiritual poverty" became the grounds for binding persons in apprenticeships. By the end of the seventeenth century, legislation pertaining to the binding out of poor children referred more to economic considerations than to deviance. After 1692, only children were subjected to the jurisdiction of family governments other than their own; poverty-stricken or wayward adults more often were placed in work-houses, almshouses, or other institutions. By the law of 1692, children "not having estates otherwise to maintain themselves" were subject to being bound out—boys to age 21 and girls to 18 or time of marriage. Although no definition of poverty was provided in the law, presumably only children in families receiving alms were considered as falling within the law's jurisdiction (Towner, 1966, pp. 422-423). Records of apprenticeships indicate a wide variety of trades: baker, chairmaker, apothecary, housewife, iron-monger, glover, clerk, weaver, tanner, potter, brickmaker, cordwainer, caulker, ropemaker, and mariner (EIHC, 1922, pp. 263-264; Towner, 1966). It should be emphasized that the apprenticeship of poor children was not a short-term arrangement but instead involved a long period of bond, often over ten years, as shown in the following cases:

> The wife of Peter Joy of Salem, fisherman, bound her daughter, Sarah Joyce, aged seven years, with her own consent, and also with the consent of her grandfather and grandmother Cascoine, and by order of the selectmen of Salem, from January 1, 1673-4, until eighteen years of age, to Mr. Joseph Porter of Salem, husbandman. . . .
>
> Charles Atwood . . . bound himself to William Baker of Ipswich, from April 11, 1687, to March 1, 1699, thirteen years, to learn the trade of a glover. . . .
>
> The selectmen of Salem, on January 22, 1694-5, bound John, son of Joshua Lyon, late of Salem, deceased, aged eight or nine years, to Mr. Joseph Capen, clerk, of Topsfield, and Priscilla, his wife, until 21 years of age.
>
> The selectmen of Salem, on August 4, 1696, bound Thomas Meshury, son of Benjamin and Margaret Meshury, both deceased, he being eleven years of age, to William Abbott and Elizabeth, his wife, of Andover, until said Thomas should reach the age of twenty-one years, to learn the trade of a weaver. [EIHC, 1922, pp. 263-264]

* * *

The Puritan Ideology of Family Government

The use of family government and the apprenticeship system as the basic means of social control declined steadily during the eighteenth century. As noted above, the function of apprenticeships to socialize and control subordinates and youth actually had begun to wane in the previous century (Bailyn, 1960, pp. 29-32). The effect of the continual loosening of familial control in the 1700s may be noted in the median age at first marriage for men, as indicated in Table 2-1. This table describes the age at first marriage for men related either by birth or marriage to heads of households in Bentley's membership list in the East Church as of 1790 (as well as the marriage of the heads themselves). The tabulation thus includes persons living outside Salem's East End. Data were available for 597 men who married between the years 1751 and 1825. The data were split into quartiles by year of marriage to provide four periods: (1) 1751 to 1775, just prior to the Revolution; (2) 1776 to 1790, the year in which the list was compiled; (3) the time of rapid growth in Salem shipping, 1791 to 1805; and (4) mainly the aftermath of the Embargo of 1808.

Table 2-1 indicates a general tendency for men to marry at increasingly later ages with the passage of time. The median for the first period, ending in 1775, was 23.9, whereas the median for the last period, ending in 1825, was 26.8. The medians, however, reflect mainly the continual spread in the age at which men entered their first marriage. The table also presents the interquartile ranges (Q_3-Q_1) for the four periods. The interquartile ranges, covering the middle 50 percent of cases, increased steadily from 2.7 years for the period 1751-1775 to 5.2 years for 1806-1825. Prior to the growth of the shipping industry, family government was still strong, and most men married between the ages of 22 and 25, just following their period of apprenticeship. By the early nineteenth century, however, family controls had weakened somewhat, and personal discretion assumed a greater role in decisions of when and whom to marry.

Table 2-1
Median and Interquartile Ranges of Age at First Marriage for Men in Salem, 1751-1825*

Time Period of Marriage	N	Median Years of Age at First Marriage	Interquartile Range
1751-1775	140	23.9	2.7
1776-1790	153	24.6	4.4
1791-1805	154	25.3	4.9
1806-1825	150	26.8	5.2

*Based on relatives of household heads listed by Bentley in 1790 as members of the East Church.

This change in age at marriage seems to represent a relaxation of the control by parents and community over adults and adolescents. As mature children took on the responsibility for their own marital destinies, family government lost its power, and individual conjugal families assumed a measure of autonomy.

Socioeconomic Characteristics and Family Composition

The effectiveness of family government in maintaining guardianship over the young is related to the composition of the family and household. The occupational structure of Salem influenced family composition. By the end of the eighteenth century, there was considerable specialization in the division of labor. Generally, three occupational classes can be identified: (1) merchants and professionals, (2) artisans, and (3) laboring classes. In the analysis, however, it was convenient to treat sea captains as a separate category, since they often were in a transitional stage from artisan to merchant. Many sea captains were simultaneously shipmasters and merchants. Customarily a portion of the cargo space was reserved for the captain's own use. Yet, in hard times, when a captain could not find a ship to command, he usually signed on as a mate or even a seaman for a voyage.

The merchants and professionals included the wealthier and more educated segments of the population. The term "trader" was used to designate the shopkeeper who ran a small enterprise, usually specializing in a single type of commodity: yard goods, or groceries, or tobacco. "Merchant" had the connotation of large-scale enterprise, diversity of goods, direct connection with a shipping business, and—perhaps most important—wealth and power. Certain professionals bordering on artisan status, such as the apothecaries in the sample studied, had amassed considerable wealth and invested funds in a variety of enterprises. For the most part professionals, like doctors and lawyers, had had a classical education in addition to training in their respective disciplines.

The artisan class included virtually all crafts (apart from the professions) for which an apprenticeship was necessary. This group included such highly skilled masters as goldsmiths and male public-school and private-school teachers, verging on the professions, as well as economically marginal occupations like baker or cordwainer (shoemaker).

The laboring class included a conglomerate of unskilled workers, including fishermen and mariners (seamen). Often the members of the laboring class had gone through an apprenticeship (usually in an overcrowded craft) but could not obtain work for which they had been trained. Possible reasons for this situation are varied: the inadequate training often given to boys from poor families, ill health, insufficient need for journeymen, or lack of capital to purchase tools and supplies. In addition, the laboring class included immigrants to the community either from Europe or other New England towns as well as ex-slaves (automatically freed when Massachusetts became a state). Together, these workers formed a class of "proletarians" by 1790.

The three occupational classes in Salem society had their origins in the federated community organization derived from Puritanism. Such an organization implies a hierarchical arrangement, with the merchant and professional class as the élite and the laboring class at the bottom. This arrangement is reflected in various ways in the family and household characteristics described below. The efficacy of family government in influencing life-chances at different socioeconomic levels seems to be related to demographic realities, some of which are explored in the analysis: (1) age at marriage, (2) length of life, (3) number of children, and (4) household composition.

The data for the analysis refer to the 238 families (and their relatives) listed as members of the East Church in 1790. This list of families offers a wide variation in socioeconomic position and provides a core of individuals for whom publications of the Essex Institute (e.g., vital records, historical collections) yielded some biographical information. In all data on occupation, birth date, date of marriage, age at death, and/or number of children were available for 943 couples, many of whom lived outside the East End of Salem.

Age at Marriage

Although a general weakening of family controls took
place, the system of family government did not collapse
entirely in the years 1751-1825. Table 2-2 shows age at
first marriage for men by occupation. Four classes of occupations are presented: (1) merchants and professionals,
(2) sea captains, (3) artisans, and (4) laborers, mariners, and
fishermen.

The data in Table 2-2 indicate that for both the earlier
years (1751-1790) and the later period (1791-1825) there

Table 2-2

Age at First Marriage for Men for 1751-1790 and 1791-1825
(by occupational class)*

		1751-1790			1791-1825	
Occupational Class	N	Median Age at Marriage	Inter-quartile Range (in years)	N	Median Age at Marriage	Inter-quartile Range (in years)
Merchants and Professionals	49	24.1	5.0	67	27.3	5.9
Sea Captains	87	24.3	3.8	60	26.6	5.1
Artisans	80	24.0	2.8	69	25.9	3.7
Laborers, Mariners, and Fishermen	46	24.5	4.3	46	26.0	7.7

*Based on relatives of members of the East Church of Salem in 1790 listed
in Bentley diary.

* * *

were appreciable differences by occupation in the dispersion of men's age at marriage. For the earlier era, median age at first marriage was similar for all occupational classes (range of 24.0-24.5 years of age). However, even then the dispersion of age for artisans was much smaller than that for the other occupational classes. The merchant and laboring classes had appreciably large dispersions (as indicated by the interquartile range). For the 1791-1825 era, the merchants and sea captains still had only slightly higher median ages at first marriage than artisans and laborers. The major differences among occupational classes in the latter period occurred in the interquartile ranges. Again the age at first marriage for artisans was more closely bunched than that for other occupations. The dispersion for the laboring class was particularly large in the 1791-1825 period. The weakening of the controls of family government thus seems to be particularly significant in the lower-class population. In contrast, the role of family guardianship remained fairly firm for the artisan class in the first quarter of the nineteenth century.

The median age at first marriage for women is shown in Table 2-3. The women described in this table are the first wives of the men in Table 2-2, and the occupational class is that of the husband; some women were married previously (and, when appropriate, their age at the previous marriage was used in the analysis). Most women married within their socioeconomic level. The women's median age at first marriage for the period 1751-1790, like the men's, showed little difference by occupational class. Similarly, the increase in median age at marriage from the 1751-1790 era to the 1791-1825 era was, again like the men's, greater for the women in the merchant and sea-captain categories than for those in the artisan and laboring classes. The gen-

*   *   *

The Puritan Ideology of Family Government

Table 2-3
Age at First Marriage for Women for 1751-1790 and 1791-1825
(by occupational class of husband)*

		1751-1790			1791-1825	
Occupational Class	N	Median Age at Marriage	Inter-quartile Range (in years)	N	Median Age at Marriage	Inter-quartile Range (in years)
Merchants and Professionals	53	21.1	3.4	58	23.2	3.6
Sea Captains	82	21.6	4.5	53	24.2	5.8
Artisans	78	22.4	3.8	48	22.3	4.2
Laborers, Mariners, and Fishermen	50	22.2	3.3	34	22.6	5.0

*Based on relatives of members of the East Church of Salem in 1790 listed
in Bentley diary; generally, wives of men in Table 2-2.

eral pattern was for the median marital age of women to
be two to four years lower than the men's, regardless of
socioeconomic status or time-period.

The dispersion of ages at first marriage for Salem
women, by husband's occupational status, is smaller than
that for their husbands. For women, however, the interquartile ranges for the merchant and artisan classes
remained low from the 1751-1790 era through the 1791-
1825 era, whereas those for the sea-captain and laboring
categories appreciably increased. The implication here is

that at least until the first quarter of the nineteenth century, parents retained strong control over their daughters' destinies; they gave greater leeway to sons. However, the general trends in the artisan family's retention of authority and in the laboring-class dissipation of family government are also reflected in this analysis.

Age at Death and Number of Children

In general, life expectancy in Salem was short. Actuaries surmise "that for the United States at the end of the eighteenth century the expectation of life at birth must have been about 35 to 40 years" (Dublin and others, 1949, p. 41). However, as the analysis in this section indicates, age at death and number of children were both related to occupational status. Death during adulthood for some occupational groups tended to occur prior to the end of the childbearing stage in the family life-cycle. This analysis also was based on relatives of members of the East Church in 1790. Since the data were most reliable for the period 1726-1775, median age at death was computed for persons and their spouses born during that time.

Median age at death, by occupational class, for Salemites born between 1726 and 1775 (and for whom data on occupation and birth were also available) is shown in Table 2-4. The median ages at death for men and women differ widely by occupational class. For men, merchants and artisans tended to live considerably longer than sea captains and laborers, with medians in the sixties rather than the forties. The low median age at death for sea captains is, however, somewhat misleading in that, as shipmasters achieved financial success, they tended to leave the sea and to become merchants. The low median age at death in the laboring class is attributable both to deaths overseas of mariners and to harsh conditions of lower-class life in Salem.

*   *   *

The Puritan Ideology of Family Government

In the 1790 era, the cause of death for poor persons aged 20-40 was sometimes given as "worn out," "atrophy," "lethargy," and a large variety of infectious diseases (to which the resistance of poorly fed exploited laborers and their families was probably low). Given these conditions, one would hardly expect to find patriarchs and effective family government in laboring-class families.

Table 2-4
Median Age at Death for Persons Born 1726-1775
(by occupational class of husband)*

Occupational Class	Men		Women	
	N	Median Years of Age at Death	N	Median Years of Age at Death
Merchants and Professionals	75	66.3	73	58.5
Sea Captains	113	49.5	98	65.3
Artisans	107	63.6	80	72.0
Laborers, Mariners, and Fishermen	69	45.2	49	63.8

*Based on relatives of members of the East Church of Salem in 1790 listed in Bentley diary.

For women, the distribution of median age at death by the occupational status of their husbands, also shown in Table 2-4, is difficult to interpret. The medians vary from 58.5 for wives of merchants to 72.0 for spouses of artisans. Compared with the men's age at death, the data for women indicate that the probability of widowhood was high except for those married to merchants; merchants tended to outlive their first wives. Wives of sea captains and particularly laborers risked 15-18 years of widowhood. Out of the 1,438 households listed in the 1790 U.S. Census for Salem (excluding 57 headed by blacks), 15.1 percent were headed by women and held no male of 16 years of age or older. The high incidence of widowhood and of female-headed households indicates the obvious absence of a strong patriarch in many families.

Table 2-5
Mean Number of Children Ever Born to Men Married for the First Time, 1751-1805, and to Their First Wives
(by occupational class of husband)*

Occupational Class	Men		Women	
	N	Mean Number of Children	N	Mean Number of Children
Merchants and Professionals	78	7.06	78	5.92
Sea Captains	121	4.93	113	4.73
Artisans	118	5.69	114	5.90
Laborers, Mariners, and Fishermen	77	4.27	78	4.60

*Includes children born in first and subsequent marriages. Based on relatives of members of the East Church of Salem in 1790 listed in Bentley diary.

The mean number of children ever born to husbands married for the first time between 1751 and 1805 (and to their first wives) appears in Table 2-5. (Some of the children were born to the women in previous or subsequent marriages.) The mean number of children is related to early widowhood. Both men and women in the sea-captain and laboring classes tended to have fewer than five children. On the other hand, artisans had about six children on the average, and the merchants and professionals, whose wives generally preceded them in death, had a mean of over seven children, presumably some of these by a second wife. The effects of widowhood and number of children in the family on household composition are discussed in the next section.

Household Size and Composition

Households in Salem of 1790 held not only parents and their children, but sometimes apprentices and servants as well. A few housed sundry relatives. This state of affairs produced a wide variation in household composition in Salem of 1790. Families utilizing many apprentices were sometimes three times as large as the poor families from which the apprentices were drawn.

Table 2-6 indicates the distribution of household size by occupation of the head of the household for 238 families belonging to the East Church of Salem in 1790 (Bentley, 1905, I, pp. 22ff.). The merchants in the sample had the largest number of persons per family (9.8), followed by the coopers (with 9.0) and the barbers (8.3). The households of merchants, who were among the wealthiest persons in Salem, often included poor relatives as well as apprentices. The coopers were in large demand at this time inasmuch as shipping was thriving; barrels were needed not only for water but also for the coastal rum-traffic. The barbers in this sample consisted mainly of branches of the Archer family—all engaged in barbering and peruke-making—with nephews apprenticed to their uncles. Even preparation for the university was based on the apprenticeship model:

In the month of June, 1782, when about nine and a half years of age, I was placed under the tuition of the late Rev. Doctor Manasseh Cutler of Hamilton (then Ipswich Hamlet) to be fitted for college, in the company of about twenty other scholars from Salem and some of the neighbouring towns, most of whom were fellow boarders with me in Doctor Cutler's family. [Silsbee, 1899, originally 1836-1850, p. 2]

Table 2-6
Number of Persons per Family in East Church of Salem in 1790
(by occupation of household head)*

Occupation	Number of Persons per Family
Merchant	9.8
Cooper	9.0
Barber	8.3
Boatbuilder	7.25
Carpenter	6.75
Ropemaker	6.75
Shoemaker	6.6
Sea Captain	6.0
Tanner	6.0
Ship Carpenter	5.75
Laborer	5.4
Fisherman	4.2
Widow	3.7
Shopkeeper (Women)	3.0

*For those families for which at least three household heads in sample had some occupation.

Table 2-6 also indicates the relatively small size of the households of the unskilled workers whose children were apprentices to artisans and businessmen. Laborers, fishermen, widows, and female shopkeepers had the smallest households. Curiously, widows were treated as a separate occupational category; they had various vocations and were sometimes dependent upon relatives and friends for subsistence.

Removing young boys from poor families may have provided a means for upward social mobility for the boys, but it also deprived their families of additional earning power and kept these families in poverty. At the same time, the long-term apprentice system provided cheap labor. By the end of the eighteenth century, the apprentice system, stripped of its role of socializing youths and controlling deviants, had become somewhat rationalized. With rationalization, blame for the deviance of apprentices was shifted more often from the master (as an expression of poor family government) to the apprentices themselves. Apprentices who misbehaved were discharged. Bentley provides an example:

> May 4, 1790. The Thief who broke into Capt Gibaut's . . . was the Son of the present Widow Elkins. His father was a man of generous humor died in the infancy of this his elder son, who was of sulky, & dishonest temper from his youth. He has been detected often in little frauds, & when apprentice to a Baker lost all his credit in the world.

The increased rationalization of the apprenticeship system also means, however, that the financial gain to the master far exceeded his costs of feeding, clothing, and schooling his apprentices (and sometimes providing them with tools). The sons of the wealthy masters, given their patrimony, were in a far superior competitive position to that of the artisans who had been apprenticed from poor families. Often poor apprentices could not remain in the trade for which they had been trained but had to accept unskilled labor or berths as mariners. This occupational instability would further decrease the ability of the laboring-class family to control its members. The trend toward rationalization of the apprenticeship system, it should be noted, occurred long after Puritanism ceased to be a vital force in the lives of Salemites.

The effect of the apprenticeship system on household composition was particularly pronounced for males under the age of 16. Here, especially, socioeconomic differences among households were found. Table 2-7, which shows some variations from the previous table, indicates that families of unskilled workers (and of widows) had less than one male under 16 per family. More affluent households had two or three male youngsters per family. Poor boys thus tended to spend most of their formative years in households other than their own. This system facilitated the persistence of the conception of family government, even in a weakened form, as covering apprentices and servants long after the initial motivations for these policies had ceased.

Despite the rationalization of apprenticeships, the master-apprentice-worker relationship remained quasi-familial. Often, in the confounding of household and business, the term "servant" was used to cover any class of workers. Indeed, workers (and especially apprentices) were considered as subordinate members of the household. They were *in* but not *of* the community. Again, Bentley's diary reveals the domestic status of many poor workers (in this case a black man):

July 25, 1793. . . . Roger, a negro Servant of Capt. Allen, attempting to remove with his fellow servant a boat from Derby's to Allen's wharf, fell into the water near the wharf.

*   *   *

The Puritan Ideology of Family Government

His fellow Servant saw him not again, but ran to his Master, & before he could be relieved, he was dead. . . . He was brought from Mrs. Allen's patrimoney, & employed upon low wages to the satisfaction of all parties.

July 26, 1793. Poor Roger was buried this afternoon, in due form, & the Negroes appeared in all order, & well clad. . . . The Coroner appeared to make inquest after the company was assembled, but it was a doubt whether he ought to have been indulged. *The Servant was in his master's service, perished in his territories*, & no suspicion was entertained. . . . that he had been abused. [Italics mine.]

Table 2-7
Number of Males Under 16 per Family in East Church of Salem in 1790
(by occupation of household head)

Occupation of Head	Males under 16 per Family
Cooper	2.9
Barber	2.3
Boatbuilder	2.25
Merchant	2.0
Ship Carpenter	2.0
Shoemaker	1.8
Ropemaker	1.75
Sea Captain	1.5
Carpenter	1.2
Laborer	0.9
Mariner	0.9
Fisherman	0.8
Tanner	0.7
Widow	0.7
Shopkeeper (Women)	0.0
All others*	1.4

*Fewer than three household heads with same occupation in sample.

In brief, by uniting the household and the economy, the Salem apprenticeship system, despite its increasing rationalization, acted to sustain the existing ideology of family government as the mechanism for maintaining the economic and political *status quo*. It was able to accomplish this action even in 1800 partly through the manipulation of household composition, which deprived the laboring-class families of supplementary workers, but it was also assisted by the high death rates of lower-class breadwinners and the relatively small number of children born in that class. The low birth rate and high death rates in the laboring class weakened family government further and made it possible for the artisans to absorb survivors as quasi family members. Hence, although economic currents may have weakened the effectiveness of the Puritan family ideology, vital birth and death rates and the manipulation of household composition made it possible for the apprenticeship system (as the foothold of strong family government) to persist.

Unbound Labor in Post-Puritan Salem

The concept of the poor as residents but not inhabitants of the federated community lingered in Salem after the American Revolution. Although the Puritan doctrine of predestination and election was no longer an overt ideology, its institutional residue still provided a basis for the social structure in Salem in the 1790s. Despite the fact that cotton-cloth manufacturing machinery had already been introduced in Essex County, the inhabitants of Salem sought to limit the labor force in order to protect local artisans. Instead of maintaining a labor surplus, they sought to banish the poor and noninhabitants or at least to disavow any responsibility for their welfare.

The Puritan Ideology of Family Government

Of the spread of manufacturing in Salem, Bentley wrote in his diary:

> September 29, 1790. Visited for the first time the Salem Duck Manufactory. It has now at work about 12 spinners, & 4 weavers. They intend to add to this number. . . . Purchased a quire of paper from the Paper Mills at Andover. They begin to manufacture good writing paper tho' not of the first qualities. They intend however to be rivals to the paper manufactory at Milton.

Bentley thus recognized the growing importance of manufacturing in Salem in the 1790s. The existence of a free labor market, however, interfered with the ideal of a tightly organized hierarchy of authority, whereby the community was responsible for the disposition of persons in the absence of effective family government.

In this situation the interests of the families engaged in craft enterprises also had to be protected. Elsewhere Bentley noted the desirability of protecting the economic interests of inhabitants:

> July 26, 1790. The question agitated before the Selectmen, whether to warn Strangers out of Town, in order to save the Town from the charges of the Poor. It is found in fact that the greater part of the whole property is in the hands of persons not Town born, & in the best streets even a majority of freeholders.

The practice of warning strangers and paupers out of town extended back to the seventeenth century. As early as 1639, the Massachusetts Bay Colony, according to the records of June 6, "ordered that the Court . . . shall have to determine all differences about a lawful settling and pro-

viding for poor persons and shall have power to dispose of
all unsettled persons into such towns as they shall judge to
bee most fitt for the maintenance of such persons and families and the most ease of the community." In the ensuing
years, the various towns sought to divest themselves of those
poor noninhabitants who they decided could not be re-
deemed. On May 11, 1695, the Court passed "a law whereby several towns could order any strangers coming within
their limits to reside to leave immediately." Inhabitants
were required to inform the board of selectmen when strangers were residing with them so that the board, if it saw fit,
could order the noninhabitants out of town (Fowler, 1860,
pp. 85-86).

The early Puritan doctrine of family government had
been based on the assumption that each "foreign" individual or family could be placed under the jurisdiction of
family governments during a trial period. This arrangement
was feasible in small agrarian and fishing villages. By the
end of the eighteenth century, however, the growth of seaports like Salem, with populations of nine or ten thousand,
brought many outsiders from different lands, many of
them seamen who had decided to remain in port and to
raise families there. The size of the population precluded
the effective operation of a family-government system. The
large mass of "strangers" facilitated the freeing of the laboring class from family guardianship. The remaining alternative for the community, derived from federal theology,
was to rid itself of the responsibility for these "strangers."
The "strangers" had become a social class rather than
merely individual undesirables.

On May 13, 1791, the selectmen of Salem issued a
warning to 261 residents and their families "who [are]
lately come into this Town for the Purpose of abiding
therein not having obtained the Towns Consent therefore,

that they depart the limits thereof with their Children &
others under their Care within fifteen days" (EIHC, 1907,
pp. 345-352). Sixteen individuals on this list were members
of the East Church and were listed by Bentley as members
of his congregation. These 16 members, mainly mariners,
carpenters, and laborers, had an average of 5.2 persons in
their households. (According to the 1790 U.S. census data,
there were 5.3 persons per family for Salem as a whole.) If
the 5.2 figure is extrapolated for the 261 "strangers," about
1,300 people would be represented by this list. Since the
entire population of Salem in 1790 was about 8,000, the
segment represented by the 261 persons warned, together
with their families, probably constitutes more than one-
eighth of the total population (as a conservative estimate).

The "strangers" warned to leave were, in general, lower-
class Americans. Of the 261 persons, 173 (about two-thirds)
were American-born. Almost all of the non-Americans were
English, Irish, or Scottish. The occupations of the "strangers"
were listed with their names and places of origin in most
cases. This information was available for 216 of the 261
persons listed and is presented in Table 2-8. Generally, the
more persons listed in a given occupation, the lower the
socioeconomic status associated with that occupation.
Mariners, laborers, and fishermen (and widows insofar as
they may be considered an occupation) represent the
unskilled workers in Salem society. Bakers, blacksmiths,
general carpenters, butchers, cordwainers (shoemakers),
and tailors were often described as poor, and they usually
left small estates. At the other extreme, clerks, school-
masters, goldsmiths, and the other occupations required
more training and education. The list of "strangers" thus
represents a segment of undesirables who in earlier Puritan
days would have been forced into the jurisdiction of other
families.

Table 2-8

Occupations of Persons Warned to Leave Salem Within 15 Days
(in 1791)

Occupation	Number of Persons With That Occupation
Mariner	67
Laborer	42
Widow	15
Fisherman	12
Baker	8
Blacksmith; Carpenter	7 each
Butcher	6
Cordwainer; Tailor	5 each
Ship Carpenter; Weaver	4 each
Cabinetmaker; Husbandman; Ropemaker	3 each
Boatbuilder; Chairmaker; Chaisemaker; Hatter; House Carpenter; Leather Dresser; Painter; Wheelwright	2 each
Clerk; Currier; Dyer; Goldsmith; Joiner; Sailmaker; Schoolmaster; Tallow Chandler; Tobacconist	1 each
Total	216

The 1791 warning given to the "strangers" to leave
Salem was not an isolated incident. At the end of the previous year, on December 6, 1790, the selectmen issued a
similar warning to the blacks of Salem. Although the notice
did not refer specifically to blacks (merely " to all the persons mentioned in the within List who have come lately
into this Town"), the list was described by the constable as
"an account of No. of Black People within the limits of the

towne of Salem." There were 99 names on the list. With families included, the list represents 274 persons (since wives and children were mentioned in the notice). In 61 of the families, husband and wife were both present; 20 men were without wives (3 of these men with children); and 14 women without husbands (7 with children). (In four instances, the first names did not permit classification as male or female.) Hence, the list consisted mainly of complete nuclear families (EIHC, 1908, pp. 93-96). (Compared with the 1791 list of poor whites, there were more black female household heads.)

The repeated warnings of 1790-1791 evidenced the persistence of the inhabitants' conception of Salem's social organization as a hierarchy of authority, with family government at its base. Since the persons warned were generally poor, the action implies that poverty denotes degradation and an absence of self-discipline. Moreover, inasmuch as the warnings included families, they carried the additional connotation that faulty family government was involved.

The significance of the lists of warnings lies in the implicit assumption of a special status ascribed to non-inhabitants and their children. Defined as "strangers," the poor outsiders and the blacks were considered as objects of exploitation: nonpersons to be banished arbitrarily. It matters little that some of the persons on these lists continued to live in Salem according to later references: e.g., Primus Grant and Lydia King appear in the Bentley diary long after 1791; Nehemiah Adams is listed as a charter member of the Salem Mechanics Charitable Society in 1817. More important is the nature of the social structure revealed in these lists: the guardianship of the organized community over its residents.

Although the extent of family guardianship seems to

have declined with the rationalization of apprenticeships, the basic conception of Salem as a federated community remained to the end of the eighteenth century. The decline in civil guardianship took place as the number of deviants and "strangers" exceeded the ability of the traditional control mechanisms to handle the problems. Even the "warnings" in 1790 and 1791 were ineffective in ridding Salem of undesirables. In this context, extrafamilial controls on family government tended to dissipate, and the conjugal family was relatively free to develop as an autonomous unit.

Problems in Family Guardianship

Family guardianship in Salem covered most traditional contingencies. Problems in guardianship arose when the responsibility for children could not be assumed by the parents or, in the case of apprentices, the masters. Lack of guardianship meant an absence of family government.

Difficulties in guardianship most notably developed in two kinds of situations: illegitimacy and the incompetency of parents. Situations covered by the incompetency of parents included death (particularly of the father), extreme poverty, or desertion by the father.

Illegitimacy and Guardianship

Illegitimacy created particularly serious problems regarding guardianship. Since there was no recognized father, the illegitimate child was not provided with a responsible member of the community as a guardian. He was therefore outside the authority of a family government that conformed with community norms. Illegitimacy indicated the failure of family government in another way as well. Since illegitimacy implied sex outside of marriage, it suggested an unnatural family condition, the failure by the girl's parents to raise her properly. Since her parents could be accused of inept family government, and she had no husband who could claim guardianship, the matter of guardianship of the mother and her illegitimate child was generally shifted to the community.

A previous section of this chapter indicated that children in poverty-stricken families were generally bound out as apprentices by the selectmen. This situation reduced the ability of these girls to repel sexual advances by masters or members of their masters' families. Besides, participating in a sexual relationship with the master (or his son) might instead provide rewards for the girl. Hence, mothers of "natural" children were sometimes already living with a family other than their own, a situation which probably increased the risk of illegitimacy. Bentley noted:

> October 9, 1792. . . . The Parson at Lynn since his degrada-
> tion has been busy with a bound servant in his Father in
> Law's family, & the girl has confessed her condition & the
> cause. She has been sent to Philadelphia with a negro man,
> but has returned to Boston, & both are in the charge of the
> Overseers.
>   Sept. 1, 1805. . . . Last night, a Crispin living in a family
> near the East Meeting, delivered herself before her time & con-
> cealed the child in a vault & went to Meeting. The child was
> found buried in ashes by the family in the afternoon service.
> The Physician pronounced the child an abortion & the girl
> was committed to the Work house where she had been several
> times. The character of these children has obliged complaints
> to the police from parents.

Since illegitimacy reflected on the family government of the girl's family of orientation, the social class of the

family played an important role in determining the consequences of illegitimacy for the girl. In lower-class families,
the effects of illegitimacy might be minimal. Among artisan-class families, however, signs of poor family government were regarded as tragic. An illegitimate child reflected
not only upon the artisan-class girl but her parents and
their ascendants and descendants as well. In this class, therefore, the implications of illegitimacy were grave.

Illegitimate children requiring community guardianship
were generally made residents at the charity house. (Of
course, sometimes illegitimacy might not come to the
attention of the overseers, and the prevalence of illegitimacy cannot be estimated.) The *Salem Vital Records* reveal
the death of illegitimate children at the charity house. For
example, on December 12, 1800, the "natural" child of
Lydia, daughter of Daniel Cloutman, was reported to have
died of convulsions at the charity house. Not all children
raised in the charity house, however, died there. Bentley's
diary contains the entry:

> March 12, 1797. . . . This G[rand] Son of Lassell, was a g.son
> of his Wife by a Crispin, & was a natural child by John Jenkins,
> whose name he bore. He was bound out from the Charity
> House to a man in Marblehead in the fishery, & was just free,
> & went his first voyage with Capt. Needham of Salem, & died
> of Small pox in the Southern States.

Incapacitation of Parents

Since guardianship was a major function in family life
in Salem, the death or incapacitation of parents was considered threatening to the Salem social structure. Without
effective family government, the traditional hierarchy of
guardianship which governed social relations would collapse. It was therefore necessary to develop institutional

means for taking over guardianship in case of the death or incapacitation of parents. Most often this guardianship was assumed by either the grandparents or the uncles and aunts. Especially in the case of a husband's desertion (and partly because of the high death rate among mariners), the mother's relatives often took on the responsibility for guardianship. Bentley records in his diary:

> June 15, 1803. This morning died Hannah Archer, Widow of Nathaniel Archer. . . . she went through great changes of life. Had a fine presence, & a strong & active mind, which she preserved till her death, at 86 years of age having outlived her own generation. . . . She took great care of two of her great grandchildren Byrnes, & received constant attention from the Derby family, particularly Patty now Mrs. Prince. . . . She had no children which survived her, but 11 grand children and g.g. children in great number. . . . [two of] which she adopted and educated.
> December 15, 1811. . . . This young man [Samuel Cheever], an only Son, married G. Osborn's daughter & was a Tanner in the Western part of the Town as the Father was at the Corner of the Common from Brown's to Winter Street. He was unsteady and went to the West Indies & the Southern states, & finally returned to Salem to die. His wife & 3 children have continued in Salem under the care of her Father and friends.
> February 17, 1814. . . . Found at John Babbidge's, four Children, a son & 3 dau. of Col. [Samuel] Archer cast upon the charity of this Tradesman, the first wife's brother. [Susannah Babbige was the first wife of Samuel Archer.] He has above 20 persons in his family.

However, at times there were no relatives available who could assume the responsibility for guardianship. Merchants and professional men considered it as part of their civic duty—their general calling to be useful in society—to assume guardianship in such instances. Bentley notes:

> Nov. 18, 1811. Last Saturday died Capt. Joseph Franks. His
> Father a Corsican & his Mother from the Island of Jersey. I
> found them in Salem when I came to it in 1783, and esteem-
> ing the integrity of the Father, who was then indigent, I took
> the expences of the Schools for the Son, Capt. Gibaut
> received him from me & educated him for the sea & his
> prospects were good. His habits for a time rendered his suc-
> cess doubtful but as they were induced by losses they were
> not unsurmountable. He had good dispositions & talents &
> was in great esteem. A long sickness & Consumption termi-
> nated his life, & he left a Wife & Child. He had acquired a
> considerable property which he lost by some adventures &
> much reduced the sums which his Father had accumulated.
> But he did not die poor & his Father with his humble cart &
> the rich donations of Capt. Gibaut will be able to render his
> wife & child comfortable.
>
> May 8, 1796. . . . Emmons Smith & Wife & Children, d.
> of his Eldest Son. This Son of Smith was named Stephen, &
> had been living long decaying in a Consumption, was by
> occupation a Rope Maker, living with Briggs & several years
> of the first of life in Danvers, with the father of Dr. Arche-
> laus Putnam, aet. 23.

It was not until the Industrial Revolution that significant changes occurred in applying the concept of family
government to most of the population. The immigration of
the Irish, French Canadians, Italians, and Poles enlarged the
free labor force appropriate for rational capitalism. Essex
County became ethnically heterogeneous, and "was no
longer Yankee but cosmopolitan. . . . A young generation
was growing up which knew little about the Puritan
Founders" (Fuess, 1956, p. 12). Under these conditions,
any attempt to impose the ideology of family guardianship
would have been futile.

Conclusion: Family and Guardianship

In Puritan Salem, responsibility for all persons in the community had been given to the family to govern in all aspects of their lives: religious, economic, personal, and educational. Adults were obligated to marry, and placing nonrelated persons under family control was accomplished mainly by the apprenticeship system. Young persons, who might be freest in moving about and changing jobs, were bound following English tradition from an early age into adulthood. Hence, the concepts of discipline and family government overrode other considerations in structuring community relationships.

As commerce developed and Salem increased in population, the feasibility of imposing responsible family government upon everyone declined. The pressure to marry shortly after the completion of apprenticeships decreased. Apprenticeships became more economically and less morally oriented, and steps were taken to drive deviant and poor families from the community in large numbers. The reaction to the decline in family government was intended to protect the traditional structure of the Salem economy and social order. Still, other developments described below precluded a successful maintenance of traditional structures.

The hierarchical arrangement of authority and personal rights in Salem contrasts sharply with the laissez-faire conception of community organization and government which emerged in the nineteenth century. Puritan society—and the basic realm of family government—aimed at the tight integration of political, economic, and religious institutions. As long as Puritan ideals persisted in dominating Salem, this tight integration of the different facets of social life fostered the viability of the traditional social structure.

The federated organization of the community stressed the importance of the conformity of family government at all socioeconomic levels to Puritan prescriptions. Those at the lower levels were particularly constrained to conform during the colonial period. The economic development of Salem, however, fostered (1) a merchant class willing to enter into risk-taking enterprises to maximize profits, and (2) the creation of a flexible, unbound laboring class to be exploited.

The data indicate an increasing differentiation of the Salem social structure at the end of the eighteenth century. The early age of death among lower-class males, the relatively small number of children left unprovided-for, the occupational differentiation in the community, the household size (with more powerful families having larger households), all suggest a change in lower-class family life toward the end of the century. Moreover, the poor families who were "strangers" in Salem could no longer find protection in the family government of the élite. The warnings to leave town can be interpreted as a disclaimer of responsibility for the poor families; henceforth, the conjugal families would be autonomous. From an economic perspective, these families constitute the unbound laboring class required by industrial capitalism, which was to emerge in Salem half a century later.

The development of a merchant class willing to take risks and the presence of unbound workers in the laboring class did not mean the immediate demise of the ideology of strong family government as the basis for the social structure. The artisan class played an important role in maintaining the stability of the Salem community structure. Here people still had a long life expectancy, fairly large families, a source of cheap labor supply in apprentices, and an interest in maintaining the old social and economic order implied by their traditional crafts.

Implications of the differentiation of Salem social structure for family organization will be explored in the succeeding chapters on economy, political life, and socialization. These chapters will focus upon the ways by which family structure, which was modeled upon the old Hebraic organization, functioned to meet the problems which arose in the economic and political life around 1800.

3

Family, Economy, and Succession

The Puritans conformed with the biblical family organization in most respects, including its system of inheritance. In reacting to the English institution of primogeniture, however, the Puritans did not restrict inheritance to a single heir, nor did they limit transfer of property only to male children. According to the Massachusetts law of 1641:

> When parents die intestate, the elder sonne shall have a double portion of his whole estate reall and personall. . . . When parents die intestate having noe heirs male of their bodies their daughters shall inherit as copartners. [cited in Calhoun, 1945, I, p. 121]

Thus, as among the Jews of biblical times (and even afterwards), the Puritans reserved for the eldest son, as the new head of the family, a double share of the inheritance, which often included the family homestead. Often, unlike Judaic practice, upon the death of a Puritan husband, the family property passed to his wife and only after her demise to the children. There was, however, considerable discretion in testation, and shares of property were distributed among male and female heirs.

The laws of succession among the ancient Hebrews passed through several stages. In an early stage of existence, the clan organization provided generally for the eldest son to inherit his father's position as leader of the family; the estate remained undivided as the property of the corporate family rather than of any individual. At a later stage, the eldest son was considered entitled to a double share not only of real but often also of personal property. The remainder of the property was generally divided equally among the remaining sons. In principle this aspect of succession was retained in Puritan society. The primary difference between Hebrew and Puritan society was in the ability of Puritan women to inherit property. In biblical Hebrew society, widows had no right to inheritance, and daughters could share in the estate only when no male heirs were present (Falk, 1964, pp. 165-170).

The division of inherited property in Puritan society seems to have had a profound effect on the relationship between family and economy. The rise of industrialization in England has been attributed in part to its inheritance practices. Habakkuk (1955) notes, "It is significant that England, the country of earliest factories and regions of industrial concentration, was the country where, with a few minor exceptions, younger children had no claim at common law to any share of their father's estate." He indicates a comparable inheritance-pattern was also responsible for the rapid development of German industry. In contrast, Habakkuk points to the Russian *mir* and to the French system of succession under the Napoleonic Civil Code as inhibiting industrialization.

The reasons given by Habakkuk for proposing a direct influence of inheritance patterns on industrialization amount to Max Weber's conditions for facilitating capitalism. Habakkuk's position is that the practice of having a single heir produces (1) an increased concentration of capital in the family lines of single heirs instead of depleting capital among heirs, (2) a highly mobile labor market consisting of nonheirs, since they have no continuing economic interest in their family's enterprises, and (3) an increase in population by the nonheirs, who become part of the industrial labor force free from traditional family influences, and who marry early and in increased numbers.

There is a question as to whether primogeniture and entailing inherited property in perpetuity were feasible in the American colonies. Opposition to primogeniture and entail came early not only in Massachusetts but also in Virginia, where English laws governing the succession of property prevailed (Morris, 1930, pp. 86-92). To be sure, lands were entailed, particularly among the English Loyalists in New England—for example, the Pepperells, who intermarried with the Sparhawk and Ropes families. However, estates in the Salem area changed hands frequently. Many Virginians also tried to circumvent English laws governing entail and primogeniture. In the decade preceding the Revolution, roughly one-sixth of all acts passed in the Virginia legislature dealt with docking entail provisions for specific estates (Keim, 1926, p. 136).

There is no evidence to suggest that the abolition of primogeniture and entail was a political issue in the eighteenth

* * *

Family, Economy, and Succession

century. Rather, primogeniture and entail were prevailing customs nowhere in Revolutionary America. In Virginia, the abolition of entail and primogeniture after the Revolution had little impact on inheritance practices. Jefferson justified his bills in the Virginia legislature to repeal entail and primogeniture on ideological grounds to prevent the perpetual accumulation of wealth in select families in a manner "which made one member of every family rich, and all the rest poor." When he introduced these bills, he met with little opposition. Because of the heavy investment in tobacco in Virginia, old lands were continually wearing out, whereupon families moved to new estates. Since entail is designed for fixed estates, not varying ones, it was inappropriate for American practices in land tenure. Moreover, in New England the abundance of cheap land made entail and primogeniture superfluous (Keim, 1926, pp. 138-154). Yet entail was slow in disappearing entirely. In Massachusetts, the Hebraic practice of a double-portion inheritance for the eldest son persisted in law until 1789; the statute governing entail was modified in 1783 (Morris, 1927, p. 47). However, the Massachusetts laws even in the early twentieth century permitted entailed estates in situations governed by common-law rules (Morris, 1930, p. 94).

Succession among the Salemites in 1790 followed the practice of dividing estates among siblings (with females included among the heirs). As a consequence, certain relationships among heirs in merchant families might be expected. First, inasmuch as much testatory discretion existed, there was often occasion for conflict among heirs. Second, following Habakkuk's reasoning, we may also anticipate that the heirs of merchants would not be highly migratory but would remain in the community and maintain an active interest in the family's enterprise. Third, we would accordingly expect among the merchant families a widespread practice of family partnerships (as opposed to stock companies) to pool resources. Fourth, because of the divisiveness among heirs, these business partnerships would be unstable. This chapter will examine data relevant to these expectations.

We also expect that, among craftsmen, the inheritance system had effects different from those of relationships in merchant families. One of the prominent traditions noted in the previous chapter was the existence of a widespread apprenticeship system, which was closely associated with family guardianship. We anticipate that the data will show the persistence of strong family relationships among those in skilled trades. The differences in family solidarity between merchant and artisan classes probably influenced the direction of economic and political development in Salem.

On the basis of the above speculations regarding the consequences of the system of inheritance, this chapter describes problems in testation, as well as some aspects of the roles of relatives as partners and as apprentices.

The Ethics of Testation

The Puritan background of the post-Revolution Salemites importuned them to act morally not only in life, but also in their testation of property to be distributed after their death. They generally conceived of property as a unifying force in family life, a symbol of success (and, initially, of divine Grace). Ostensibly, such signs of success should be distributed among all heirs to permit each of them to accumulate capital. Inheritance could thereby provide a basis for further investment rather than for living out an indolent life. According to Main (1965, p. 283), "there existed a general admiration for the man who acquired an estate" by personal achievement.

Yet the emphasis on the accumulation of property acted paradoxically to create conflict and disunity in families. The basis for disunity lay in the practice of willing unequal shares to different heirs, as well as in the difficulty sometimes encountered in determining the exact worth of real and personal properties. Where considerable sums were involved, jealousy and competitiveness ensued. This disunity inhibited the pooling of resources among the various heirs to capitalize entrepreneurial ventures adequately.

The will of Richard Derby (EIHC, 1861, pp. 163-164), an abstract of which is presented below, illustrates various kinds of property disposition that could lead to family disunity: rough estimates of worth, uneven distribution among children, cancellation of debts, mere confirmation of earlier gifts, and testation of property to grandchildren.

In the name of God Amen. I Richard Derby of Salem in the County of Essex in the Commonwealth of Massachusetts Merchant on this twenty seventh Day of October in the year of our Lord seventeen hundred eighty three, do make my last Will & Testament in manner following.—First I give unto my well beloved wife Sarah Derby all the Household Furniture Goods &c. which she brought to me upon and after our Inter Marriage.—I also give her my Chariot and two Chariot Horses; also the sum of £100 lawful money annually, while she shall remain my widow, also my negro Child Peggy.—I give to daughter Mary Crowninshield, the House in which she lately dwelt now occupied by Joseph Moses with the Land under & adjoining thereto, it being nearly opposite the Meeting house in the East Parish, which I purchased of Christopher Babbage's Heirs;—and I confirm to her all the Household Furniture & Plate which I gave her about the Time of her marriage, estimated at £400 lawful money;—And I also give said Mary my

House called Ropes house in which she now dwells;—Also the debt of £400 lawful money due on Book from her Husband Capt. Crowninshield;—also my negro Girl named Cate, with her apparel, all of which I estimate at £3,400. Item. I give Daughter Martha Prince wife of Doct'r John Prince the Mansion House wherein she last resided at Salem and all Household Furniture & Plate I gave her about time of marriage;— Also my negro man Ceesar;—also £1000 in specie to be paid within six months after my Decease all which I estimate at £3400. Item, I give my grandchildren John Gardner, Sarah Gardner, & Richard Gardner, the Children of my Daughter Sarah Gardner dec. to each the sum of £1000, which together with Household Furniture & Plate are estimated at £3400.—Item, I give to son Elias Hasket Derby the land belonging to his Warehouse on which it stands extending from the street by my wharf about sixty six southward, to the notch in the wharf, with the Passage way & Dockage westward of it.—Item, I give the Remainder of my Estate, to son Elias Hasket one third part, to son John one third part; and the remaining third including the Mansion house, wharf and Buildings thereon, which I gave to my son Richard late deceased, to his sons Richard, Samuel, Jonathan & Charles, and to his Daughters Lydia, Mary & Betsy the aforesaid mansion house, wharf, &c., estimated at £2000 lawful money:—I appoint sons Elias Hasket & John Derby, and, son in Law John Gardner 3d, Executors of this my last Will and Testament. [Probated Dec. 3d, 1783]

1. To his daughter Mary Crowninshield, Richard Derby gives (a) the house in which she had lived, (b) the Ropes house (where she then lived), (c) a cancellation of a £400 debt owed by her husband, and (d) a servant girl. These, in addition to a confirmation of his wedding gifts to her, Derby estimates at £3,400. He then equates this legacy with that given to her sister Martha Prince: (a) the mansion house in which she had resided, (b) a man servant, (c) a confirmation of wedding gifts, and (d) £1,000 in cash. The

equivalence of the two endowments hinges on whether the
second house given to Mary is actually worth £600.

2. The legacies awarded to his sons, given Richard
Derby's wealth, are larger than those for the daughters.
Both sons are given equal residual portions. But in addition,
he leaves his elder son some business property without estimating its worth. Derby could apparently justify unequal
distribution between sons by the custom of leaving a double portion for the eldest son.

3. Derby discriminated among the offspring of his
deceased children on the basis of their parent's sex. To the
three children of his deceased daughter, Derby left £1,000
each; together with household furniture and china, presumably wedding gifts, the estimated total worth of this
legacy was £3,400—the equivalence of the award to his
daughters Mary Crowninshield and Martha Prince. To the
children of his sons, however, Derby left a mansion house
as well as business property, which he estimated at only
£2,000.

Interestingly, Derby appointed his sons and son-in-law
alike as executors with equal status, thereby suggesting the
equivalent status of son and son-in-law in kinship organization. Also worth noting is that he did not appoint his wife
Sarah as executrix of his estate, although many wills did
follow this practice. Perhaps his choice of executors fore-
stalled some conflict over inequalities in the distribution of
the estate.

Another notable aspect of the Derby will is the absence
of a charity bequest. If one had to live morally, so should
one die morally. Bentley remarks bitterly about another
will: "April 25, 1817 . . . . Not a Cent was left for any charity foreign or domestic, nor has one been promised by the
male heirs who will have what the world will never count,
the greater part of the estate." We can only surmise Bentley's

opinion of the Derby will if we also take into account the enmity between the Federalist Derby family and Bentley's close friends, the Republican Crowninshields.

Although conflict over wills might not initiate bad feeling among heirs, inequities in legacies might occasion the eruption of latent smoldering hostilities. Given the Puritan-derived prescription of living as secular "saints," people tended to suppress many perceived personal slights, suspicions, jealousies, and disappointments. The wide discretion in testation, limited only by the requirement of a widow's share, apparently fostered much overt conflict when underlying hostility was present. While the uncertainties of life demanded solidarity between kin, the emphasis on the personal accumulation of wealth sometimes created disunity.

The Bentley diary reveals a variety of occasions of family disruptions over wills. Bentley's entries stress the role of wills in precipitating overt conflict among relatives already disposed to do battle. He sees problems arising out of testation as indicators of immorality rather than mere disruptions in family unity:

April 27, 1817. . . . The shameful inequality of the [Hannah Manning] will prevented the heirs & branches of B. Hodges & Mary Boardman from any notice. . . . Everyday tells us that the disproportion is great & it is now believed that George & Gamaliel H. will share above 100 th.D. while the others, more deserving but less intriguing, will share only 8 th. . . . We think with horrour of these transactions . . . we see too little moral sense, &c.

December 17, 1818. As they [the Harthorne family] have successively gone from life they have left serious quarrels about their property. The last Mary made a will but it was not found & her Brother took the mansion house & made one Alb. Gray his heir. Lately upon selling the house in a neglected part of the furniture in a private drawer was

* * *

Family, Economy, and Succession

found the will. Notice was given. The will was in favour of
Nancy [a sister]. Suffice it to say there was much talk on the
subject, but the night ended the dispute. The house was
entered, the will was seized, & has since for a second time
disappeared. A more extraordinary set of folks seldom are
grouped together.

January 15, 1818. The discovery of a will . . . in the
possession of a kept mistress of G[eorge] C[rowninshield]
has occasioned much sensation. The vitious part of the Community think it a debt of justice, tho they hardly dare com-
mend the form. The Enlightened part of the community see
the discharge of dividing the property by law, while the
Mistress divides by Will.

Problems encountered in testation suggest a situation in
which there was ample opportunity to express built-up
suppressed hostility, jealousy, and other disruptive family
sentiments. One consequence of these disruptive sentiments is a segmentation of the lineal-descent group.
Whereas sometimes descendants of a wealthy merchant
might be inclined to pool their resources, hostilities over
inheritance could, perhaps just as often, create factions
among relatives. Over a series of generations, the enmity
created might splinter the networks of extended families.
The following section on family partnerships provides
some indication of the extent to which the disunity among
relatives appeared in the merchant class.

Relatives as Partners

Kinship played an important part in the development of
commercial enterprise in New England. Throughout the
seventeenth century, "commercial ties were best secured by
the cement of kinship or long friendship. . . . Brothers, sons,

and 'in-laws' continued as agents of their English relatives" (Bailyn, 1955, p. 87). The necessity of trusting others in distant ports, without communication over long periods of time and without the ability to apply sanctions for dishonesty, facilitated the use of relatives in shipping ventures.

Moreover, New England merchants in expanding their trade during the seventeenth century had to cultivate networks of correspondents in England, the West Indies, the European continent, and different American communities. In doing so, they often depended on relatives and friends to establish relationships of reputation and trust throughout the trade area. Just as American merchants were frequently offshoots of English trading families, occasionally American families also spread out over their sphere of trade. The Winthrop family, which itself had relied on family ties in England for its sponsorship in commerce, had representatives in the seventeenth century in various New England towns, as well as in the West Indies. The Boston Hutchinson family was in a similar position. The networks of family ties were loose. "Relatives operated in a constantly shifting series of combinations, as partners, as agents, or merely as customers to each other" (Bailyn, 1955, pp. 87-89).

The use of family representatives in a trade network implies the dispersal of family members over a wide area. This distribution of the family rests on the utility of nonmaterial elements in business enterprise: reputation, trust, knowledge about the market. The dispersed family members are thus not dependent upon the sharing of a divisible estate to maintain relationships; the more representatives there are in this trade network, the greater the probabilities of finding profitable markets. With the use of family members as trade representatives in foreign ports, the motivation is high to maintain strong family solidarity.

*   *   *

Family, Economy, and Succession

The presence of family networks of trade representatives, however, seems more appropriate to a primogeniture
system of succession than to a system based on partition
of estates. In primogeniture, the heir can maintain control
over the network through his manipulation of the estate.
The siblings rely upon him for underwriting credit and for
a major part of capital investment. Their inheritance is
symbolic: the family reputation. In a system of estate-parti-
tion, however, control is more difficult. This was especially
so when communication over long distances was poor: family
members in the outposts of trade would have had little voice
in decisions regarding the use of their portion of the estate
in the family enterprise. Accordingly, family members sharing in the estate tended to remain near the headquarters of
the family enterprise and could therefore participate in decision-making. The English system of maintaining family solidarity through the development of trade networks thus did
not seem to work efficiently in the New England situation.

According to Bailyn (1955, pp. 101-102), most early
overseas merchants of New England had been (or had families who had been) tradesmen in England. This origin seems
to have influenced their ambitions—quite apart from their
Puritan convictions. "For centuries the goal of the London
business men had been to prosper in trade, marry into a
family of higher social standing, provide themselves with
landed estates, and begin the process of transferring their
family from the status of tradesmen or merchants to that
of gentlemen." Accordingly, the New England merchants
invested heavily in land, which could be transferred to their
children. Their business assets were generally intangible:
reputation, number and quality of commercial correspondents, investments in ships and voyages. However, with large
land-holdings, they aimed to achieve a secure status for their
families.

The flaw in the reasoning of merchants with ambitions to found family lines of gentry derives from the fact that, although they followed the English model of social mobility, they were not in England. The English system required primogeniture, or at least nondivisible succession. Under the American system of inheritance, the landed estates would eventually be broken up. Accordingly, the organization of merchant families eventually became adapted to the unique character of the American society. In a sense, merely by becoming successful merchants, these men and their families had already reached the pinnacle of New England society. This emphasis on achievement as a basis for social position implies, however, that the instability of alliances among merchant families was endemic to the system itself.

Family Partnerships in Salem

The extent to which business partnerships were associated with family ties after the American Revolution can be suggested by examining the Salem registry of ships. Inasmuch as shipping was the main industry of Salem in the period 1790-1810, the ownership of ships provides an index of general business arrangements. Ships were owned not only by merchants, but also by artisans, bankers, professionals, and sea captains in the community. In addition, although banks and insurance companies in Salem had been incorporated, there were no corporate bodies listed as owners of ships; the registry therefore indicates the importance of partnerships in the Salem economy and provides an opportunity for examining the kinds of family ties involved in these partnerships. For example, partners in vessels Elijah Porter "and Seth Low who married his sister were Druggists in Salem and afterwards in New York" (EIHC, 1864, VI, pp. 207-208).

* * *

Family, Economy, and Succession

The years 1800-1810 represent the decade during which Salem shipping was at its peak. With the War of 1812, Salem declined as a port. Morison (1941, Appendix V) indicates that after reaching a high point in 1810, the tonnage of shipping owned in the Salem district dropped permanently. In the years from 1790 to 1800, the total number of ships in the Salem deep-sea fleet increased only slightly, from 124 to 138. However, the tonnage rose from 13,726 to 19,636 with the construction of larger vessels to permit profitable Asiatic and Middle Eastern trade. By 1810 the tonnage almost doubled (36,272), and there were now 221 ships in the Salem registry (Phillips, 1947, p. 3). (Note: Although there are technical differences between ships, brigs, schooners, and sloops, distinctions between these classes of vessels will not be made in this analysis.)

The lists of Salem ship registers for 1800 and 1810 have been compiled by James Duncan Phillips (1944; 1947). Phillips reports his procedure for collating the 1800 list as follows:

This list has been obtained by taking the names of all vessels during the year 1800 entering or leaving Salem, or reported as Salem vessels spoken at sea or in other ports, and checking them back against the Salem ship registers. Most of the vessels mentioned are found readily in the registered list, a few are not and some of the numberous Sallys, Pollys, and Betseys have been difficult to identify. Vessels not found in the registers have been excluded on the assumption that they were erroneously called Salem vessels or were small coasters enrolled but not registered. . . . The owners' names are taken from the ship registers which give the last owners before 1800. [Phillips, 1944, p. 261]

The 1810 list was compiled by Phillips in a somewhat different manner:

The list was prepared by drawing off the names of all vessels entering or clearing from Salem in 1810 mentioned in the *Salem Gazette* from January 1 to December 31 and adding to it the names of all vessels spoken or reported in foreign ports which are stated to be "of Salem." It was assumed that any vessel not mentioned in the paper during the year had ceased to be "of Salem" even if the Register of Vessels gave no clue to her having ceased to be a Salem ship. [Phillips, 1947, p. 1]

In the analysis, problems of identifying relationships of partners were occasionally encountered. One problem was the existence of several related persons, all with the same first and last names. Usually there were various clues to the identity of the appropriate person: mention of partnership in the historical collection (EIHC) or in Bentley's diary, age in 1800 or 1810, occupation (especially listing as a merchant), identity of the other partners (e.g., known enemies), and so on. In a few instances, notably in the case of John Derby, the choice was somewhat arbitrary; since the other partners were either sons or sons-in-law of Elias Hasket Derby, it was assumed that the John Derby listed was also a son, rather than a brother or a cousin. The second problem encountered in the identity of related partners was the listing of partners with the same last name, but for whom there was no indication in the historical collections or vital records of the nature of their relationships. Seven such cases were encountered and were classified as of unknown relationship.

Family Partnerships in 1800 and 1810

The distribution of individual owners and partnerships for deep-sea vessels in the Salem register for 1800 and 1810 is shown in Table 3-1. In 1800 single owners held 44.6 percent of the ships, and in 1810 their percentage rose slightly to 49.8. In both years the largest individual owner was William Gray, with 16 ships in 1800 and 12 in 1810 (Phillips, 1944, p. 262; 1947, p. 3). "He took no interest in other men's ventures and allowed them none in his. It was no doubt this non-cooperative attitude that added to Gray's unpopularity in Salem" (Phillips, 1947, p. 3).

In the light of William Gray's unpopularity in Salem, his career seems noteworthy in that (1) it probably approximates a "calling" as implied by Weber's spirit of capitalism, and (3) Gray represents the exception rather than the rule in his avoidance of partnerships (cf. EIHC, 1863, p. 147).

William Gray, born in Lynn in 1750, moved to Salem in 1765 to become clerk of one of the Gardners and then of Richard Derby.

As soon as he was of age, he owned part of a vessel with Mr. Derby—his share being the result of his savings while a clerk. . . .

> After the war of the Revolution had ended in the peace of 1783, he extended in foreign trade with varied success. Once he had lost all—but kept on, and regained, with unimpared credit.
>
> His high integrity, and reputation for sagacity, gave confidence to many retired persons in Salem, Marblehead, and other towns, who placed large sums with him at a low rate of interest, in preference to public institutions at a higher rate. . . . When William Gray left Salem [for Boston], his property was valued at three millions of dollars, on a careful estimate. . . . About that time, he owned and loaded more than forty vessels at his own risk: he was besides a large underwriter, taking almost desperate risks, in the face of British and French seizures. . . .
>
> Mr. Gray was simple and unostentatious in his habits, an early riser. . . . It was his nature to help those whom he thought were trying to help themselves. . . . As his sons came of age, he gave each ample means, that they might start and

* * *

Guardians of Virtue

work for themselves. . . . Regardless alike of the denuncia-
tions of the public press, and the scornings, batings, and bad-
gerings of the junto . . . , he stood for his country. [Anon.,
1848, pp. 18-19]

Table 3-1
Ownership of Deep-Sea Vessels in Salem Register, 1800 and 1810

	1800		1810	
Ownership	N	%	N	%
Total vessels	138	100.0	221	100.0
Individual ownership	62*	44.9	110	49.8
Partnerships	(76)		(111)	
a. Unrelated persons	46	33.3	51	23.1
b. Involve known or presumed close relatives	30	21.8	60	37.1

*Of the 62 ships owned by individuals, 16 were the property of William
Gray.

The epitome of the Weberian "ideal type" Protestant
merchant, William Gray formed few close personal ties. His
independence from family and friends is suggested further
by his switching political allegiance from Federalist to
Republican, thereby exposing "himself to all the virulence
of invective. . . . [by] his former professed friends" (Bentley, 1911, III, p. 501). In brief, although Gray exemplified
"the spirit of capitalism," he was considered deviant in his
familial, political, and economic affairs; in contrast, other
merchants placed much importance on family solidarity,
political loyalty, and the maintenance of business partnerships.

Merchants who endured large financial losses without
partners were indeed in a precarious position. Generally

cargoes were underinsured, and ships were sometimes unin-
surable (since their condition was so bad that they had difficulty getting clearance from harbor-masters). For example,
Benjamin Ropes was an independent merchant and ship-
owner who went bankrupt. Although he had a sister who
married a merchant, as well as numerous cousins, some of
them wealthy, he carried on his business independently of
them. Ropes wrote in 1810 (EIHC, 1955, pp. 114-115):

> I had the Vanity to think, that I had as many friends as any
> one, but I find it all a Delusion, for when the Hours of Dark-
> ness & Distress came on, they liek the Diciples, all forsook
> me and fled, & those I had befriended the most ware my
> worst Enemies. Now what shall I do, having lost & given up
> all my Property, look at me a sight anough to melt a hart of
> Stone, with a Family of Small Children, without a Dollar
> warewith to Support them, House & all gone, No Friend that
> care to give me any Assistance, or imployment, What Shall I
> do, famly a Suffering, myself no Peace, almost Driven to
> Distraction, but I will Trust in God for Vain is the help of
> Man.

Family partnerships played a prominent role in Salem
shipping. The largest change in the distribution of partnerships between 1800 and 1810 was in the percentage of
ships owned, at least in part, by relatives. In 1800 only
21.8 percent of the total ownerships involved partners who
were relatives, while in 1810 the percentage of ships in
which the partnerships included relatives rose to 37.1. Inasmuch as the proportion of individual owners remained
fairly constant from 1800 to 1810, the rise in partnerships
involving relatives meant a corresponding drop in ownership of ships by unrelated partners. However, it must be
remembered that in a community of 8,000-10,000, where
there was a tight network of business relationships, much

intermarriage occurred among these families; therefore most families were at least distantly related in one way or another. The families most heavily involved in the ownership of vessels were the Derby family in 1800 and the Crowninshields in 1810. Either in family partnerships or individually, in 1800 the group of Derby heirs including Benjamin Pickman and Nathaniel West owned nine vessels totaling about 2,070 tons; in 1810 the Crowninshield family controlled 12 ships of over 2,800 tons altogether. The destinies of the Derbys and the Crowninshields will be discussed later.

Relatives involved in partnerships in deep-sea vessels registered out of Salem in 1800 and 1810 are shown in Table 3-2. The unit of analysis in Table 3-2 is partnerships rather than persons. In the construction of the table, one individual in the partnership was designated as EGO and his relationship to other partners was ascertained. When the partners were of different generations, the older person was chosen as EGO. In the table, the 32 partnerships between relatives in 1800 represent 51 persons, and the 62 partnerships in 1810 consist of 97 persons, with a few individuals related to several of their partners. In some cases, the partners owned several ships. Altogether, the 51 related partners in 1800 account for 37.4 percent of the total number of persons owning vessels in 1800, and the 97 related partners in 1810 comprise 42.4 percent of the owners. Since the percentage of ships involved in partnerships between relatives rose faster than the percentage of relatives among owners, the change from 1800 to 1810 indicates an increase in the average number of ships per partnership and a greater pooling of relatives' resources in 1810 to capitalize shipping.

The composition of partnerships is also indicated in Table 3-2 in terms of relationship to the person designated

* * *

Family, Economy, and Succession

Table 3-2

Partnerships of Relatives Owning Ships Registered Out of Salem in 1800 and 1810 (by relationship)

Relationship of Partners to EGO, by Generation	1800		1810	
Collateral with EGO				
Br	13		18	
SiHu	5		4	
WiSiHu	1		1	
FaBrSo	1		—	
FaSiSo	—		1	
MoBrSo	—		2	
FaBrDaHu	—		1	
Total		20		27
Descending from EGO				
So	3		15	
DaHu	3		2	
BrSo	1		4	
BrDaHu	—		2	
DaHuBr	—		1	
WiSiSo	—		1	
SiHuSiSo	1		—	
Total		8		25
Other		2		5
Unknown		2		5
GRAND TOTAL		32		62

as EGO. In 1800 over half (19/32) of the partnerships with relatives consisted of brothers or brothers-in-law, and about a fifth (6/32) were sons or sons-in-law. By 1810, the kinship base of partnerships had broadened: only one-third (22/62) of the partners were brothers or brothers-in-law, and an additional one-fourth were sons or sons-in-law. However, the increase for sons is especially notable: there were five times as many father-son partnerships in 1810 as in 1800.

The partnerships involving cousins and nephews, by blood or marriage, rose during the 1800-1810 period from one-tenth (3/32) to one-fifth (13/62). The presence of four EGO's brothers' sons (nephews) in 1810, as compared with one in 1800, is accounted for by men without children of their own. Distant relatives and partners with the same last name, but for whom the exact relationship could not be determined, increased roughly in proportion to the total growth of partnerships involving relatives (from 4 to 10).

The partnerships among relatives in deep-sea vessels were generally unstable. Of the 32 partnerships in 1800, only eight pairs remained in 1810, aside from the Crowninshield brothers. Four of the eight partnerships were brothers, two EGO's sisters' husbands, one son, and one brother's son. Partnerships among all classes of relatives, as well as nonrelatives, were thus highly ephemeral and were usually tied to a specific ship rather than to a fleet.

In general, the findings pertaining to partnerships among relatives in deep-sea vessels registered out of Salem reveal the following:

1. The proportion of ships involving partnerships between relatives increased from 1800 to 1810. Since this period was one of rapid expansion of the shipping industry of Salem, the increase seems to represent a rise in the pooling of family resources to capitalize overseas ventures. As long as the tonnage of ships had remained small, individuals could finance them with a minimum of outside sources. However, as Salem became heavily involved in worldwide trade, additional capital was required.

2. The broadening of the familial financial base is

reflected in the wider circle of kin who were partners in 1810, as compared with that in 1800. The percentage of partnerships with cousins or nephews, by blood or marriage, doubled during the decade (from about 10 to 20 percent of all partnerships involving known kin). There is some indication that partnerships were a symbol of cohesion. It was noted earlier that William Gray's avoidance of partnerships apparently contributed to his unpopularity. The data also indicate that partnerships frequently followed political lines. Federalists tended to form partnerships with other Federalists, and Republicans with other Republicans. The names of Federalists like Derby, Dodge, Orne, Pickman, Pickering, Thorndike, and Forrester tend to appear together, while the Republican Crowninshields, Hathornes, Silsbees, and Stones are generally associated in the partnership lists (see Whitney, 1958, pp. 31-32). The large proportion of related partners (and the increase in percentage from 1800 to 1810) and political allies, hence, suggests the importance attributed to family and political solidarity in Salem commerce.

3. In both 1800 and 1810 brothers constituted the largest category of related partners. This tendency is consistent with both their pooling of resources and show of solidarity. Many of the brother-partners were sea captains, and the demonstration of solidarity had more than a symbolic significance. Often voyages, especially to the Middle East or the Orient, would take many months and sometimes a year or two to complete (with numerous ports of call along the way, involving the purchase and sale of several cargoes on a single voyage). With such long voyages, there might be no communication or knowledge about the success or extent of cargo purchasing or selling. Consequently, the captains had complete autonomy and had to be trusted to act with integrity and in the shipowners' best

interests. Family ties were used to insure honesty and common financial interest. Even when neither brother sailed,
the pooling of their shared inheritance symbolized, at least
for the duration of their partnership, family solidarity. This
solidarity is also reflected in the number of sisters' husbands in partnerships. In letters and diaries, brothers-in-law
are often referred to merely as brothers. In addition,
brothers-in-law would share in the inheritance either
through the sister or in their own right, as in the case of
Nathaniel West, who married Elizabeth, the eldest daughter
of Elias Hasket Derby, and who was made "an heir in full"
(Bentley, 1911, III, p. 261).

    4. The greatest change from 1800 to 1810 with regard
to related owners was the increase in proportions of sons
and brothers' sons in ship partnerships. These two categories of partnerships are related in that partnerships with
brothers' sons were formed only when EGO had no children of his own. The brothers' sons then became heirs.
There may be several bases for the increase in the number
of sons as partners. First, the rise in the number of ships
afforded more berths for sons as sea captains, who might
then be taken on as partners. Second, the amount of capital
required for the larger ships of 1810 necessitated the pooling of a son's funds with those of his father. Since the sons
would eventually inherit these funds anyway, the father-
son partnerships did not change patterns of succession (and
would meet with little opposition by anyone). Symbolically,
the father-son partnerships were also meant to portray high
family solidarity.

    5. The family partnerships were relatively unstable, in
that most did not persist from 1800 to 1810. This finding
suggests that despite the intention of family partnerships
to symbolize solidarity, the competition for limited funds
and the potential conflict among partners tended to break

up families into nuclear (or conjugal) units. In addition the uncertainty of the progression of voyages apparently created such risks and anxiety over these risks that kinship solidarity could not be maintained. It may also be noted that family partnerships were often formed informally and thus could be easily dissolved. Nathaniel Silsbee, merchant and later U.S. Senator, reports:

> In February, 1812, my brother Zachariah on his return from Europe concluded to abandon a seafaring life and to try his fortune on shore, and from that time the adventures and speculations of either myself or my brothers, were for account of all three of us; not, however, as "co-partners" but for the account of each, in such proportions as were from time to time, agreed on between us, according to our respective means. [Silsbee, 1899, originally 1836-1850, p. 29]

Instability of family partnerships is explored further in the next section.

Decline of Family Partnerships

The instability of family partnerships in Salem suggests the problem of whether such arrangements are inherently ephemeral or whether the decade between 1800 and 1810 presented some unique difficulties in maintaining these partnerships. It is possible that such events as the 1808 embargo precipitated the breakup of partnerships between relatives. This possibility, however, is inconsistent with the actual increase in the proportion of family partnerships from 1800 to 1810, and with the appearance of most ship-owners in both the 1800 and 1810 registers, although with different partners.

The course of family partnerships can be ascertained by examining the destinies of some of the major merchants.

Such an examination reveals two general problems in family businesses: (1) deviant behavior not compatible with the rationality required in commercial enterprises, and (2) failure to maintain either an effective division of labor among family partners or a sense of solidarity.

Deviant Behavior. Some family partnerships failed to survive because of the deviant behavior of family members. Since shipping entailed high financial risk, business partners had to place a high value on each other's judgment and dedication to the enterprise. Any behavior leading to distrust or suggesting unreliability was detrimental to the family partnership. In an obvious instance, Samuel Archer included his mother-in-law as a partner in some business dealings of questionable ethics, and soon afterward he left Salem hurriedly for a southern climate. In another case, Captain Edward Allen "employed [in a broad sense] Brothers in law who have not rewarded his confidence & . . . he was surrounded by the demands of his creditors. . . . His wife . . . has consigned all her property to the creditors of her husband & the whole estate disappears" (Bentley, 1911, III, pp. 509-511).

Dissolution of family partnerships or inability to form them tended to occur, paradoxically, where there was a strong patriarch who either created the family business or acted as its leader. In these families, the sons may have been overwhelmed by their father, for they often had severe personality problems (see Saveth, 1963). The firm patriarchal authority, which seems to have facilitated coordination between family relationship and industry in artisan families, apparently was detrimental to family and enterprise in the merchant class. A few examples are presented below:

1. From William Bentley's diary concerning the family of Simon Forrester:

Family, Economy, and Succession

December 6, 1807.... A son of Capt. Simon Forrester, of the
same name, upon his return from the East Indies plunged into
the Ocean & perished. He had long been in habits which could
not promise much for his future years.

April 11, 1816. A succession of events has directed the
public attention to the fate of family of Forrester.... By
uncommon success in business he became one of the
wealthiest men in the Country. He was a man of business, of
strong passions, & such a man as his condition might readily
form. Upon his prosperity he became intemperate, & severe
in his family & irregular.... One of his sons leaped from the
windows of a Cabin into the sea. Another has died this day
in fits after a few hours illness.... The whole eccentric.

2. From Bentley's diary, concerning the sons of
Edward Allen:

October 18, 1818.... Henry Allen [died] aet. 28, youngest
son of Edw. Allen.... had been master of a Vessel.... He
became intemperate & finally was in the Marine Hospital....
He was calm & resigned to his fate. A pleasant youth but his
brothers all went the same way.

3. From Bentley's diary, concerning the son of Captain Edward Gibaut:

August 11, 1805.... This day reached us ... the account of
the death of John Gibaut, Esqur. Collector for the port of
Gloucester. We had long been in expectation of this event....
He was born in Salem, 1768, & pursued his preparatory studies for the University at the Dummer Academy at Newbury
under the noted Master Moody.... He spent several years in
this Academy & entered Cambridge University in 1782....
He was a modest, diligent, & well informed youth at his
admission.... When he took his first degree in 1786 he was
a Scholar, a Gentleman, & a man of sterling worth. But by

becoming a student, his modesty degenerated into a reserve which confined his acquaintance, & feeling an aversion to the labours of society in the learned professions he was allured by the wealth of the families around him to try the seas. He went several voyages to the East Indies, but soon indulged the hopes of retirement. After his return in 1795, he undertook the Survey of Salem, its Harbour, & Islands. . . . Thus brought into notice he became the object of the just solicitude of his friends but his inconquerable habits still pursued retirement. With Capt. G. G. Smith, with whom he lived in the greatest intimacy, & in company with whom he had performed several voyages, he purchased the farm & Mills lying toward Anasquam in Gloucester . . . he established himself at this place . . . we obtained [for him] the Office of Collector in Gloucester. For a few months his ambition overcame his obstinacy of his habits but soon finding that he had a trusting man in Mr. Rogers, his Deputy Collector, he gave up application, & gradually decayed untill he sunk insensibly into Death having passed the 37 year of his age. . . . Thus termined the life of a Man who had all the talents for usefulness & all the aid of friends with a settled aversion from all the habits of business, public life, & of an intercourse with the world.

Problems in Organization. The dissolution of family partnerships may occur for organizational reasons: (1) the failure to maintain an effective division of labor among the partners, or (2) the inability to sustain a sense of solidarity sufficient to overcome conflicting interests, personal differences, or possible distrust among the partners. The Crowninshields and the Derbys illustrate these problems. The Crowninshield brothers maintained a strong sense of solidarity but could not, in the face of the 1808 Embargo, keep an effective division of labor; the Derby heirs were not sufficiently unified to sustain a cooperative enterprise.

In the Salem shipping industry, the Derby family pre-
dated the Crowninshields, and had in fact employed the
Crowninshields as sea captains. In historical perspective:

> Timothy Orne had dominated Salem's pre-revolutionary trade,
> Elias Hasket Derby her commerce until 1800, and William
> Gray her overseas trade until the Embargo [in 1808]. But
> demanding a large share of Salem shipping after 1800 was
> the firm of George Crowninshield and sons.
>
> Old George Crowninshield had been pursuing a modest
> trade since the revolution, but with the retirement from the
> sea around 1800 of his five sons, the family firm expanded
> furiously. John, Richard, Benjamin W., Jacob, and George
> Jr., all had been sea captains at an early age, mostly for the
> town's other merchants. After their homecoming, how-
> ever, Richard became the firm's financier, John its foreign
> representative in Bordeaux, while the others directed the
> Salem counting-house. Jacob and Benjamin W., it must be
> noted, made most of the family commercial decisions.
> [Whitney, 1958, p. 2]

In 1800 the Crowninshield family had an interest in
only four ships, with a total tonnage of 1249. With the
profits from their shares as captains and from the firm's
ships, the *America* and the *Belisarius*, the Crowninshields
broadened their investments. They purchased more ships,
hired more men, speculated in land, and built warehouses
and their own wharf. By 1805 their holdings increased to
12 ships with a tonnage of over 2,900. However, the
Embargo brought some reverses. In 1810, the Crowninshield family holdings were reduced to 9 ships. After the
repeal of the Embargo in 1809, "the Crowninshields never
revived their old East India trade. . . . In haphazard fashion
they experimented with a variety of ventures to many
European ports. . . . The firm dissolved in June, 1809, with

Richard and John each becoming independent operators.
The two Georges and Benjamin W. remained together and
sustained a reduced commerce" (Whitney, 1958, p. 117).
In 1816, William Bentley reported in his diary:

> November 21, 1816. Mr. John Rice, who has lately married
> the youngest d. of Capt. G. Crowninshield, is to remove we
> are told to Philadelphia immediately. John, the son, is gone
> southward it is said with a view to an establishment. Richard,
> who went to New York & married & became bankrupt & then
> returned & erected at great expence buildings for a Cloth
> Manufacture, has the plan of another southern visit.[1] It is
> uncertain what the present Minister of the Navy [Benjamin]
> will do. George is expending a fortune upon a hermaphrodite
> Brig, which he is preparing for a visit to Europe, in a manner
> to us before unknown as to expence & project. [Note: George
> died soon afterward.] The property of the family is neglected
> here & the branches of the family divided. Not one was at the
> solemnisation of the late marriage. . . . What will be the fate
> of this family, which Jacob led to fame & property, time
> must explain.

The division of labor established in the early years of
the Crowninshield firm was dissipated as the brothers
accrued other interests. Especially with the Embargo, the
family partnership was ineffective in making rational decisions, and the interests of the brothers were diverted to
other fields: politics, government service, leisure, and conspicuous consumption. Although the personal solidarity
among the Crowninshield brothers remained long after their
business arrangements were dissolved, this solidarity was
ineffective in maintaining their partnership without a
rational division of labor.

[1] In 1830, a son of Richard Crowninshield committed a murder and then
hanged himself in his jail cell (EIHC, 1958, p. 155).

Family, Economy, and Succession

The decline of the Derby family partnerships cannot, however, be attributed to the 1808 Embargo. Their dissolution began much earlier. Whitney (1958, pp. 14-15) writes:

With the death in 1799 of Elias Hasket Derby, one of America's richest and greatest merchants, his estate was splintered and divided among many heirs. The Derby hegemony in Salem gradually vanished after 1800 until by 1810 they owned only five vessels, each in conjunction with many other merchants. A spirit of irascibility characterizing the public life of the younger Derbys hastened the family's loss of influence. There are reports of Hasket Derby's intemperance on public occasions and Hersey Derby's frequent brawling. Several disputes over their estate became very embarrassing.

The sharing of the Derby estate itself created much dissension among the sons and sons-in-law. In 1803, Nathaniel West, a son-in-law who had been made an heir on an equal basis with Elias Hasket Derby's sons, separated from his wife "after a long quarrel between West and his wife's brothers over the division of the Derby estate. In particular, Hasket Derby had fought West's claim to the Derby Danvers farm." Earlier, in 1800, they "had engaged in a bloody fist-fight on Derby wharf" (Whitney, 1958, p. 93).

By the middle of the 1800-1810 decade, the Derby family began to disband, migrating along with other Federalists to Boston. Bentley (1911, III, p. 234) reported, "The family have lost their influence in the loss of their Father." As of June 1806:

Benjamin Pickman, "King" Derby's son-in-law, advertised his property for sale . . . and was known to be leaving for Boston. Richard and John Derby had already moved there as had their three sisters. Even Elias Hasket Derby Jr. was shortly to migrate to Londonderry, New Hampshire. [Whitney, 1958. p. 94]

* * *

Since family partnerships rely upon a sense of solidarity and a cooperative organization of talent, the divisiveness among the Derby heirs made such an arrangement impossible. At the base of this lack of solidarity was the division of the Derby estate among a large number of heirs—too large to sustain a viable arrangement—with only peripheral ties to the business; there were too many conflicting interests for effective, rational decision-making. The network of family partnerships could not be protected from dissolution without the presence of a strong patriarch; however, as noted earlier, a strong merchant-patriarch often was detrimental to the personality development of his sons. Thus, either way, family partnerships were unstable.

The breakup of the Crowninshield and Derby family partnerships suggests that, given the system of shared inheritance, the number of heirs eventually becomes too unwieldy to sustain effective control over their division of labor or to maintain a strong sense of solidarity. The problems in the organization of family partnerships in Salem may have been aggravated by such events as the 1808 Embargo, but they seemed to have been generated even without external crises. Family partnerships—particularly between heirs—despite their symbolism of solidarity and their maintenance of the family resources, thus appear to be inherently fragile. Despite the symbolism of solidarity, family partnerships seem to herald the breakup of extended families.

Relatives as Apprentices

The familial basis for apprenticeships in the Salem of 1790-1800 is indicated in the narrative by Benjamin Ropes (1772-1845) (EIHC, 1955, p. 105):

* * *

Family, Economy, and Succession

> When About Sixteen years of age She [Benjamin's Mother] put
> me to my uncle Samuel Ropes [FaBr] to Learn the Coopers
> Trade Keeping my Brother at home to help support the Family.
> I was to serve two years She finding me Board & Clothing. I
> intended to have lernt my Brother the Same Trade after I had
> served my time & laboured at Jornimans Imployment a suffi-
> cient time to be capable of so doing.

Yet the system whereby sons were apprenticed to relatives fostered family relationships markedly different from
the incorporation of heirs into business as partners. Partnerships depend for their success upon the sharing of a
finite amount of capital and on developing a division of
labor and a sense of solidarity to utilize this capital effectively. Successful enterprises based on family apprenticeships, however, depend upon the transmission of skills in
service or manufacturing. Since skill, unlike capital, is not
a finite commodity, the number of apprentices does not
diminish the estate portions, but may actually increase the
family standard of living. Only after apprenticeships have
been completed do problems of competition emerge. At
this point, the extent to which family skills will persist into
the succeeding generation is contingent upon such factors
as proficiency and the size of the market.

The extent of proficiency in a skill seems to have significant consequences for the persistence of a trade in a
family over generations. In crafts requiring lesser skills and
providing small financial returns, occupational turnover
over generations was greater. There was, in addition, little
impetus for leaving the community; it was simpler to
change jobs and be near relatives in case of need.

The size of the market also seems important as a determinant in the persistence of apprenticed skills in a family
over generations. Insofar as Salem and other towns in Essex

County provided relatively small markets in 1790, journeymen often opened their shops in neighboring communities. In this manner, those in skilled trades generally established networks of kin throughout the area. This residential distribution offers a contrast to the tendency for merchant families, depending mainly on shared capital, to cluster in shipping centers. Residentially splintered, highly skilled masters tended to confine apprenticeships to their own children and to their nephews.

Three artisan families—the Archers, the Moultons, and the Beckets—are described below to illustrate the influence of skill on kinship ties and residential distribution. Although the Archer family had been engaged in various occupations, in the 1790-1800 period, many were engaged in barbering and peruke-making, a peruke being a form of wig. The second family, the Moultons, specialized at this time in goldsmithing and silversmithing; they were in the jewelry and silverware business. The Beckets were shipbuilders over several generations. All three families show signs of high solidarity but in different ways.

Figure 3-1 presents the known occupations of members of the Archer family from the mid-seventeenth to the nineteenth centuries. As for other relatively poor families, coverage of the Archers in the historical collections is spotty. Not all family members or their occupations are known. However, the figure indicates some general patterns of occupational transmission from one generation to the next.

The earliest known Archer, Samuel, who died in 1667, was a carpenter, as was his son Samuel (1634-?); the other son in Generation II, John (1638-1693) was a cooper. In Generation III, cooperage was continued, but one son, Jonathan (1671-1746), had also been apprenticed as a cordwainer (shoemaker). The third generation had no carpenters. Generation IV saw a continuation of cooperage and cordwaining, but other occupations were also introduced: mariner, peruke-maker, and fisherman. By Generation V, cooperage and cordwaining had disappeared; there was now a tailor, and peruke-making and barbering became the dominant occupations, with three cousins in these trades. Generation VI had master mariners as well as small-time traders. The sixth generation had its peruke-makers and barbers, in addition to a cordwainer and cabinet-maker. Finally, the sparse information on the seventh generation of Archers reveals a trader, a ship chandler, and a school-master. With minor exceptions, members of the Archer family remained in the Salem environs. The most notable exception was Samuel (1763-1815), a confidence man who left hurriedly for the West Indies.

The pattern of occupational transmission in the Archer family is indicated schematically in Figure 3-2. In this figure, the occupations are designated by letters. Related occupations have been grouped: woodworker (carpenter, housewright, cabinet-maker); unskilled (mariner, fisherman, laborer). The following patterns are discernible:

1. The skilled occupations in the Archer family seem to have had a life span of three generations at most. Coopers and peruke-makers fell into the three-generational pattern. However, cordwainers and carpenters spanned only two generations. Of course, during this period, perukes fell out of style, and other means of livelihood had to be sought.

2. The occupations covering three generations involved cousins. For the coopers, the succession consisted of (a) John (1638-1693), (b) his son Benjamin and his brother's son Jonathan, (c) Jonathan's son Nathaniel. The succession for the peruke-makers was (a) Samuel (1707-1756), (b) his son Samuel and his brothers' sons—both named Jonathan, (c) his grandson Samuel (1763-1815) and his nephew's sons

Figure 3-1
Known Occupations in the Archer Family

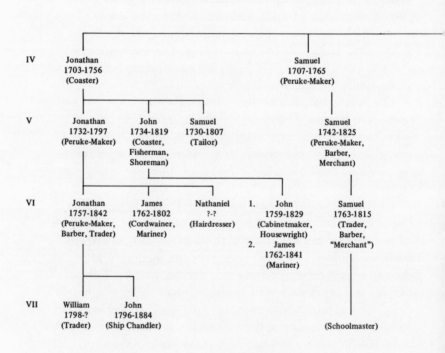

Generation

I

II

III

IV   Jonathan   Samuel
      1703-1756   1707-1765
      (Coaster)   (Peruke-Maker)

V   Jonathan   John   Samuel   Samuel
    1732-1797   1734-1819   1730-1807   1742-1825
    (Peruke-Maker)   (Coaster,   (Tailor)   (Peruke-Maker,
                Fisherman,   Barber,
                Shoreman)   Merchant)

VI   Jonathan   James   Nathaniel   1.   John   Samuel
    1757-1842   1762-1802   ?-?   1759-1829   1763-1815
    (Peruke-Maker,   (Cordwainer,   (Hairdresser)   (Cabinetmaker,   (Trader,
    Barber, Trader)   Mariner)   Housewright)   Barber,
                                      2.   James   "Merchant")
                                        1762-1841
                                        (Mariner)

VII   William   John
    1798-?   1796-1884
    (Trader)   (Ship Chandler)   (Schoolmaster)

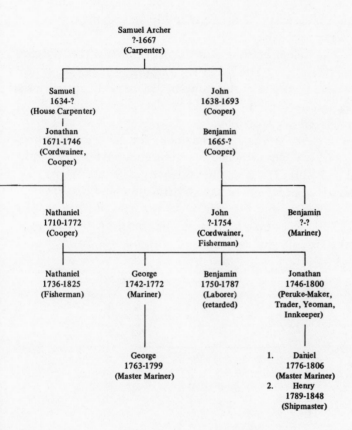

Samuel Archer
?-1667
(Carpenter)

Samuel
1634-?
(House Carpenter)

John
1638-1693
(Cooper)

Jonathan
1671-1746
(Cordwainer,
Cooper)

Benjamin
1665-?
(Cooper)

Nathaniel
1710-1772
(Cooper)

John
?-1754
(Cordwainer,
Fisherman)

Benjamin
?-?
(Mariner)

Nathaniel
1736-1825
(Fisherman)

George
1742-1772
(Mariner)

Benjamin
1750-1787
(Laborer)
(retarded)

Jonathan
1746-1800
(Peruke-Maker,
Trader, Yeoman,
Innkeeper)

George
1763-1799
(Master Mariner)

1.   Daniel
      1776-1806
      (Master Mariner)
2.   Henry
      1789-1848
      (Shipmaster)

* * *

Jonathan (1757-1842) and Nathaniel. The lateral kinship ties maintained by the apprenticeship arrangement were thus fairly extensive.

3. As Salem became a major port, more of the descendants of Samuel (?-1667) left their apprenticed occupations to become involved in the shipping industry. Eventually the Archer family turned to the sea-trader, shipmaster, and other related occupations.

In contrast to the Archer family, the most outstanding feature of the Moulton family, whose occupations are indicated in Figure 3-3, is not the diversity of occupations (for all known occupations are in goldsmithing and silversmithing and jewelry) but the residential pattern. William Moulton, born 1720, was a goldsmith and silversmith in Newburyport in Essex County and later moved with his son Enoch to

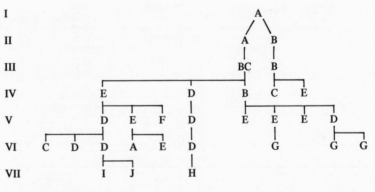

A = Woodworkers: Carpenter, Housewright,
    Cabinetmaker
B = Cooper
C = Cordwainer
D = Peruke-Maker, Barber, Hairdresser
E = Unskilled: Mariner, Fisherman, Laborer

F = Tailor
G = Master Mariner
H = Schoolmaster
I = Trader, Merchant
J = Ship Chandler

Figure 3-2
Schematic Representation of Known Occupations
in Archer Family (Figure 3-1)

Marietta, Ohio. However, his other son, Joseph, remained in Newburyport. Joseph's four sons all became goldsmiths and silversmiths, and while Abel and William remained in the hometown, Ebenezer (born 1768) moved to Boston and Enoch (born 1780) to Portland, Maine. The Newburyport business was carried on by William's son Joseph (born 1814), and Joseph, in turn, maintained the Newburyport line through his sons William and Edward (born 1844). The general pattern among the Moultons was that excess sons, having

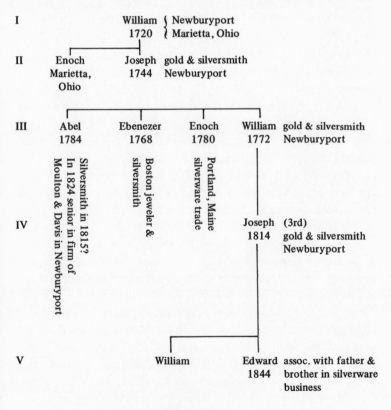

Figure 3-3
Occupations in Moulton Family

achieved proficiency in smithing silver and gold, would go into business in a different market, and a dispersed kinship network was developed (Belknap, 1927, pp. 106-107).

The nature of the craft in which kinship was involved obviously influenced the dispersion of artisan families. In contrast to goldsmithing, shipbuilding was a cooperative venture, requiring a rational division of labor and a specialized workplace. The Becket family maintained a shipbuilding tradition in Salem for over a century. Those Beckets who did not engage in shipbuilding went to sea, and the daughters of Beckets married either shipmasters or shipbuilders. The Beckets were highly skillful; some of their ships (such as the *America*) were unusually swift and maneuverable and were extraordinarily successful in privateering.

Figure 3-4 shows six generations of Beckets in the shipbuilding industry in Salem. Although other Beckets may also have been engaged in shipbuilding, the records in published Essex Institute material is incomplete for them. In Generations I-III, prior to the American Revolution, relatively few Beckets were shipbuilders. The fourth generation was active during the period in which Salem emerged as a major port, and six sons and sons-in-law of William Becket (?-1783) were building ships. However, mental illness plagued the family of William; his sons Retire and James confined themselves to their homes for years, and his son-in-law Thomas Rowell "from domestic vexation" deserted his wife and children. (Not surprisingly, Retire was bankrupt.) Another son-in-law, Benjamin Hawkes, formed a shipbuilding firm of Hawkes and Babbige, with John Babbige (Generation V), his wife's first-cousin-once-removed. John Babbige's son Benjamin (1793-1879) carried on the family occupation. By this time, Salem had declined as a seaport, and the Beckets and the Babbiges dispersed.

* * *

Family, Economy, and Succession

The three families—the Archers, the Moultons, and the Beckets—illustrate how the nature of the craft affects the stability and extensiveness of kinship solidarity. The Archers were selective in screening out relatives in somewhat unstable crafts: cooperage, shoemaking, perukemaking, and barbering. Yet, by choosing nephews rather than all their own sons as apprentices, they maintained a laterally extensive kin group, despite the restriction of transmitted occupations to two or three generations. The Moultons, however, with their more valuable family property, did tend to confine the transmission of skills to sons. The network created by the Moultons was residentially dispersed to avoid competition. On the other hand, the Beckets, in a craft which required the integration of the work of specialists, not only sons, but also sons-in-law, nephews, and more distant relatives were brought together. In this situation, the incapacitation of some Beckets merely shifted the functions of others, and the family craft survived through the continued concentration of kin in the workplace and through a division of labor. Unlike merchant families, artisan families could sustain an effective division of labor through a series of generations.

In the inheritance of skills rather than money, a major determinant in the persistence of family solidarity and enterprise was the degree of skill of the family craft. As a form of family property, the craft seemed to create a guild-like organization within the kinship group. The solidarity between the male relatives was then, like the patriarchal Judaic tribes, the mechanism by which a strong web of kinship was maintained. Likely, industrialization in Salem meant not so much the elimination of experienced artisans from the labor market as the downgrading of the particular skills as valuable family property. Only then had sons to move away from the family occupation into competitive,

Figure 3-4
Shipbuilders in Beckett Family

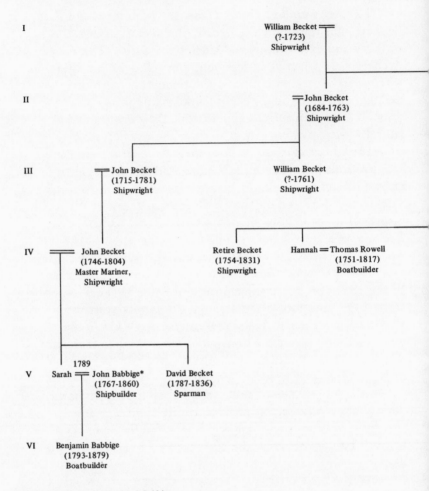

*Shipbuilding firm of Hawkes & Babbige

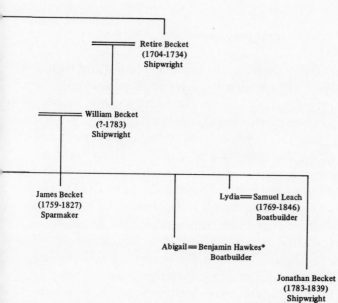

Retire Becket
(1704-1734)
Shipwright

William Becket
(?-1783)
Shipwright

James Becket
(1759-1827)
Sparmaker

Lydia══Samuel Leach
(1769-1846)
Boatbuilder

Abigail══Benjamin Hawkes*
Boatbuilder

Jonathan Becket
(1783-1839)
Shipwright

but more lucrative work opportunities (see Thernstrom, 1964).

Conclusion: Precariousness of Patrimony

The relationship between the Salem economy and family in the 1790-1810 era seems to have been influenced strongly by rules of succession. In Salem society, succession involved not only the inheritance of material property but also, given the apprenticeship system, the transmission of craft skills. The material estate was obviously fixed in size, and the practice of dividing it seems to have stimulated competitiveness and conflict among the heirs and the development of enterprise through the formation of family partnerships (rather than stock companies). Poor judgment as well as lack of cooperation affected the destiny of all partners. In England, where primogeniture predominated, unrelated heirs could maximize enterprise and minimize the risk by forming stock companies. In Salem, however, with the smaller amount of capital to invest because of the division of estates, pooling funds in a family partnership was a more feasible form of business enterprise. As a consequence, the Salem merchant families were driven to undertake many commercial ventures which they might have avoided under stock-company organization. The fragile family-partnership—as much a symbol of solidarity and trust as a commercial enterprise—spurred them to hard work in entrepreneurship.

In contrast to enterprise which relied upon pooling capital, that which was based on the transmission of crafts did not suffer the limitations of capital, but depended upon the organization of skills. Since skills were not divided on transmission to the next generation, there was no overt

competitiveness among family members. Instead, the kin-
ship-networks among artisans resembled the English trade-
networks in some ways. In both cases, the coherence of
family members was based on the inheritance of nonmaterial assets. For the Salem artisan family, the nonmaterial
assets consisted of special occupational skills; for the
English merchant family, these assets included family reputation and commercial contacts. The nonmaterial (or symbolic) aspects of family estates provided a basis for
maintaining interdependence and solidarity among brothers,
cousins, fathers and sons, and uncles and nephews.
Another similarity between the English merchant and
Salem artisan families was the central role of ties between
men in sustaining kinship solidarity. In artisan families, a
strong bond tended to develop between master and apprentice when they were closely related through kinship as well.
Moreover, the guardianship by the master would cement
ties with his apprentices' parents, who often were the
master's brothers or sisters. In English merchant families,
the maintenance of networks of business correspondents
required the retention of goodwill and trust on the part of
the male relatives involved. Hence, the findings suggest that
where kinship-solidarity was derived from a nonmaterial,
symbolic estate, as contrasted with a material estate which
was fixed in size, it tended to create strong, persistent
bonds among relatives who profited from it. The extrafamily authority associated with constant dependence on
kin and the masters of apprentices detracted from the
ability of the conjugal family to establish itself as an independent unit (cf. Ariès, 1962).

The findings in this chapter indicate that merchant
family members were placed in an ambiguous position. The
system of succession fostered conflict among the heirs and
tended to break up extended families into conjugal units.

Yet, simultaneously, entrepreneurial capitalization and risks encouraged the pooling of family resources and efforts. Salem commercial partnerships among relatives, although widespread, were generally unstable and fragile in contrast to the ties created by the apprenticeship system. Family partnerships were vulnerable to problems in the organization of a division of labor and especially to difficulties in maintaining solidarity. Still, these business partnerships did foster the development of enterprises which might not have been possible without family solidarity. Above all, the use of family ties, personal friendships, and political positions as bases for business partnerships made it possible in post-Revolutionary Salem to maintain a stable social structure in the face of flexible business connections.

4

Family, Politics, and Marital Alliances

The Puritans' use of the biblical family model seems to have had important consequences for the relationship between family and political life in the Salem of 1790-1810. In ancient Hebrew society, the connection between familial and community authority was close. The house (*beth*) was an extended-family unit under a patriarch. The *beth* included the patriarch's own wives and children, his sons' families, servants, and strangers under his protection. Related houses constituted a *mishpacheh*, based on clan organization. The *mishpachim* were bound together into a tribe (*shebet*), and together the tribes constituted a nation. The kinship basis for nationalism was thus based on a unity of religion, family, and political community. Although the early Puritans had a looser arrangement among families, they attempted to create a similar unity.

This quest for unity of religion, family, and political community led to a strong interest in government affairs among Salemites. Leading families in Salem even after the Revolution were deeply involved in political affairs. Those merchant families with a long history in Salem tended to be Federalists, élitist in spirit, and leaders in the social life of the community. The newer families, sometimes with different ethnic or religious backgrounds, were kept outside the circle of old families and often were Republican in their politics. In commenting on Nathaniel Hawthorne and his isolation from the circle of wealthy families, "which rigorously maintained the distinction of class and whose entertainments were splended and their manners magnificent," George Batchelor (1948, originally 1887, pp. 72-73) comments on "the law of blue blood in that old provincial town" at the beginning of the nineteenth century:

> At least four distinct castes may be noted in Salem society. First the blue blood; which was strictly confined to the descendants of early colonists of gentle blood in England. They were governors, judges, officers in the English army, clergymen, and such as in England would write themselves down as gentlemen.
>
> Second, there were old colonial families which came down from the English yeomanry, soldiers, farmers, and servants. . . . There were families, neighbors for two-hundred years, friends, too, bound together by many a common interest in business, in politics and religion, meeting often and cordially, and yet no man of one family ever crossed his legs under the other's mahogany, nor did any daughter of the one ever pass the threshold of the other's drawing room on any day of high ceremony. . . . And yet outside of Salem now many of the second-class are as rich and famous as the others.

Family, Politics, and Marital Alliances

A third class who had a better chance of social recognition were born elsewhere, and drawn to Salem by its opportunities, had brought remarkable energy, great abilities, or
ripe culture to engage in commerce or one of the learned professions then maintained on a higher level than is now common anywhere in America. These men of native force (and
ancestry often obscure or not aristocratic) were among the
most important actors in the brilliant years of Salem. . . . If
the first comers were not educated men, their sons were
usually sent to Harvard College and scores of college gradu-
ates were always to be found in their society.

A fourth class consisted of the many who, coming from
other towns, settled down to earn a comfortable living at
various trades with conspicuous success. Before manufac-
turers came in with Irish and French-Canadian operatives,
this class gave great intelligence and solidity to the common
life of the people.

Now it was possible to lapse from the circle of the old
families, but almost impossible to climb into it.

Although one might quarrel with the specific classes
designated by Batchelor, his classification reflects the perspective of the inhabitants of Salem. His viewpoint indicates the presence of an élitist ideology which governed the
social structure of Salem about 1800. Given the close connection between family and politics, the class structure was
reflected in government:

Political leadership in established towns like Salem had long
been the province of the rich, educated, and articulate. The
prominent family provided, nominated, and elected candidates for political office. A candidate's name mysteriously
appeared in the local newspaper, and shortly afterwards he was
elected by a few citizens assembled in a town meeting. . . .
This mode of political behavior determined the nature of
political parties. The poor and middle classes ignored poli-

tics, and, if they did participate, it was under the direction of
their betters. [Whitney, 1958, pp. 19-20]

The geographical distribution of the population in
Salem reflected the political and class structure of the community. The Federalist merchant families toward the end
of the eighteenth century began to move to the West End
of Salem. The eastern section of Salem, with its wharves,
tanyards, and ropewalks, was Republican and attracted
many of the poorer migrants. Whereas the West End was
dominated by the Derby and Pickering families, the East
End held the Crowninshields. The fact that the founder of
the Crowninshield family was not of English origin, but
instead was German, appears to have played an important
role in the family members' exclusion from Federalist cir-
cles, in their espousal of unpopular causes, in their general
opposition to the Derby family, and in their precarious
position in Salem society generally. The polemics of the
Federalists centered on Jacobinism, Deism, and the democracy proposed by Republicans. Representing the Republicans, George Crowninshield had argued that some natu-
ralized foreigners in Salem have a right to vote. However,
the Federalists pointed out that invariably "foreigners
were French, bloody, and Godless" (Whitney, 1958, p. 10).

The factionalism in the merchant-professional class,
symbolized by the Federalist-Republican split, extended to
many facets of Salem life. The merchant families generally
forced their employees to vote for the "appropriate" party.[1]
Federalist merchants (e.g., Pickman, Derby, Gray, Orne,
and John Norris), generally had more employees than did
the Republicans. William Gray alone had more than 300
workers. Employees and artisans who were dependent upon

[1] The situation in nearby Newburyport was similar with regard to deference
voting (Thernstrom, 1964, pp. 37-41).

the large merchant families were thus forced to take sides. Other institutions were also affected: when the Republicans under the Crowninshields established a Republican bank which "signified independence from control of their finances by the persons who most deplored their rise," the Federalists retaliated by forming their own insurance company. There was a separation of Republican from Federalist cliques even in concerts, dances, and ceremonial events (Whitney, 1958, pp. 30-32; Hehr, 1964a, 1964b).

It is to be expected that when close ties exist between political organization and family, a situation is created in which alliances are developed, and families take sides in this factional conflict. This state of affairs is conducive to familial control over marriage, and especially to the formation of marital alliances. As marital alliances achieve importance in the social life of the community, special significance is given to relationships with affines (Farber, 1968). Leading families in these factions may then engage in intermarriage with families of similar political persuasion and in first-cousin marriage.

The confounding of political activity and marital alliance may have consequences which are contrary to particular economic and family interests. The alliances formed by some families against others would tend to precipitate crises. Instead of devoting their energies to diligence, thrift, and profit-making, leading families sometimes diverted financial and personal resources to petty bickering and to legal and political battles. Moreover, the necessity to maintain political alliances interfered with financial dealings and created uneconomical obligations between employers and the employees whose support was required at election time. Such battles took on ridiculous proportions at times:

Late in 1801 George Crowninshield was squabbling over a right of way on land at the head of the old Crowninshield

*   *   *

wharf. When his [Federalist] antagonist, the widow Ward, built
a fence from her house to the water's edge limiting access to
this wharf, George Crowninshield at the head of a band of
hardy axmen chopped the fence down. William Gray,
Mrs. Ward's brother-in-law, hailed Crowninshield into court,
where, despite his plea that the land along the water was
common land, he was ordered to pay damages. In addition
to achieving a victory for Elias Hasket Derby, Jr., who was
Mrs. Ward's uncle and who had inspired the construction of
the fence, Gray also secured a grand jury ruling that Crowninshield be indicted for inciting riot. This grand jury stood
eight Republicans to twelve Federalists, reported Jacob, and
[it] therefore believed, with the *Gazette*, that the fence had
fallen "a victim to the levelling rage of Jacobinism." . . . A
decision was postponed until 1806. [Whitney, 1958, p. 33]

In fact, Whitney reports that "occasionally the [Crown-
inshield] sons speculated on whether business suffered on
account of their father's preoccupation with lawsuits"
(Whitney, 1958, p. 33).

The Crowninshield-Derby feud was concluded in 1806 by the
settlement of the riot case brought against George Crowninshield involving the Ward fence. It came before the state
Supreme Court in April, 1806, after a long history of hung
juries and party strife. Gray and Hasket Derby had consis-
tently led the prosecution, and they had repeatedly called
upon their Federalist friends to testify against the Crowninshields. Now the court ordered a *nol prosequi*. . . . "We con-
sider it a sort of triumph," wrote Jacob [Crowninshield], for
the case had been dismissed "to the extreme mortification
of the Derbys & Wards & your other Federal friends."
Never again were the Crowninshields dragged into court;
the Derbys had given up. [Whitney, 1958, p. 94]

As petty as many battles between families were, they

helped to separate the social worlds in which these families moved; they formed the basis for personal identification, political philosophy, and distinction between friends and enemies. Consequently, the political alignments molded business relationships and fostered the creation of familial networks.

The remainder of this chapter deals with marriage in the context of the political structure of Salem. As the basic social units governing the conduct of individuals, families formed coalitions with other families to attain power and access to resources in the community. To the extent that certain families held or desired a powerful community position, they had to pay particular attention to the formation of alliances. The dominating merchant and professional families were highly motivated to establish these coalitions; the pauperized lower class had little reason to concern itself over marital alliances. The succeeding sections of this chapter pertain to (1) the relationship between political and familial alliances, (2) the different kinds of family networks symbolized by first-cousin marriages in the merchant-professional and artisan classes, and (3) the contrast in the nature of marriage in lower-class and in merchant-professional and artisan families.

Political and Familial Alliances

The creation of marital alliances along political lines can be illustrated by a description of prominent Federalist and Republican families. The role of marital alliances in stabilizing political alignments was especially pronounced in some families active in local politics. Whitney (1958, p. 15) notes that:

Marital alliances widened the scope of friction between the Derby and Crowninshield families. "King" Derby's sons-in-law included Benjamin Pickman, Jr., John Prince, and Nathaniel West, all members of large and prominent [Federalist] families. The Crowninshields were connected by marriage to the Silsbees. Most important, these family alliances had an intimate relation to the hierarchy of the Salem political system. For the Derbys and Pickmans had long been Federalist leaders, and the Crowninshields and Nathaniel Silsbee were future chiefs of the Republicans.

Strong alliances had been created between some families long before the Revolution. The Sparhawk family had been loyalists during the Revolution and through various marital ties created connections with leading Federalist families afterwards. In 1755, Priscilla Sparhawk married Judge Nathaniel Ropes, who "was loyal at heart to the dynasty under which he had grown to manhood, and to which he owed his official standing, and could not at once bring himself to recognize the fact that the Royal Commission he was holding was destined to be one of the last ever issued to an Essex County Justice. . . . He clung to the misguided dynasty of the day, and to its supporters" (EIHC, 1904, p. 12). Numerous bonds existed with other Federalist families. The son Nathaniel Ropes (born 1759) married Sarah Putnam in 1791 and then Elizabeth Cleveland in 1803. A daughter, Abigail (born 1761), married William Orne in 1780. Another daughter, Elizabeth (born 1764), became the wife of Jonathan Hodges in 1788, and a third daughter, Jane (born 1767), the wife of Samuel C. Ward in 1790. It may be noted also that the elder Nathaniel's mother was from the Federalist Pickman family.

The Sparhawks and the Ropes were not unusual in their patterns of marital selection. Other Federalist families also tended to intermarry, and their first-cousin-marriage rate was generally high. In the genealogy of the Nichols family, the names of other Federalist families tend to recur. For example, Mary Nichols (born 1750) married Archelaus Putnam in 1775. Her brother Andrew (born in 1757) married his first cousin Eunice Nichols (FaBrDa). Andrew's son John (born 1780) married Emma Putnam, and his son Andrew [jr.] (born 1785) married his cousin (FaBrDa) Ruth Nichols. (When Ruth died, he then married Mary Holyoke Ward.) His brother Abel (born in 1792) married Sally Putnam. (The relationship between Emma and Sally Putnam is unknown; however, both were from Danvers.) Another Abel Nichols of Danvers, apparently the son of Abel and Sally, married Catherine Sparhawk Peele, thus tying the Nichols, the Putnams, and the Sparhawks into the same network.

Like the Nichols family, the Holyokes showed many connections with other Federalist families. Early in the history of Salem there were connections between the Holyokes and the Putnams and the Pynchons. Later, Edward Augustus Holyoke, the son of President Edward Holyoke of Harvard University, married Judith, the daughter of Benjamin Pickman, and their daughter Susanna (born 1779) married a member of the Ward family.

The complexity of relationships created by intermarriages in a small group of related families seems to make it easier to lump the family members together in a single class—e.g., the Sparhawk family or the Ropes family—rather than to try to sort out the tangled web of specific relationships.

To be sure, not all children were married within the confines of their parents' political world. Daughters of merchants might marry sea captains employed by their families, or, because of a surplus of women, a promising artisan.

Still, a sufficient number of children did marry within the political cliques of their parents to sustain tight-knit class and political divisions in Salem.

One of the practices which interfered with the tendency of families with similar political views to form marital alliances was the marriage of a sea captain (or an apprentice) to his employer's daughter. Occasionally the marriage took place against the wishes of the parents. This was the case in the marriage of Simon Forrester, a Federalist, to the daughter of Daniel Hathorne, a Republican. However, sometimes parental objections were independent of political views, as when Nathaniel West married the daughter of Elias Hasket Derby despite paternal objections, even though West, like his father-in-law, was a Federalist.

At times, factional splits developed after marital alliances had already taken place. This development occurred between the Derbys and the Crowninshields. As the Crowninshield family became prominent, much conflict erupted between the two families. The Derbys had employed Crowninshields as sea captains, and the elder George Crowninshield and Elias Hasket Derby had married each other's sisters. (The son George Crowninshield died unmarried.) However, by the time George's sister died in 1799, the split between the two families was so profound that none of the Crowninshields attended her funeral. There were, however, other marital ties between the Crowninshields and the Derbys. Figure 4-1 shows that Benjamin, the son of George and Mary Crowninshield, married Mary Boardman, a granddaughter of Mrs. Derby's brother John Hodges. To some extent, marriages seemed to have been used by the Crowninshields as a form of social climbing. For example, Jacob Crowninshield married the daughter of John Gardner, who had married Jacob's mother's sister

(MoSiDa), a member of the Derby family. (John Gardner was a fervent Federalist, and the Gardner genealogy shows many alliances with other prominent Federalist families.)

As shown in Figure 4-1, the Crowninshields and the Silsbees were related in a variety of complex ways. Mary Crowninshield married Nathaniel Silsbee (U.S. Senator). Her brother Benjamin W. (Secretary of U.S. Navy) was married to Mary Boardman. The sister of Mary Boardman, in turn, was married to Nathaniel Silsbee's brother Zachariah. However, the Boardmans married both Federalists and Republicans. Another sister, Elizabeth Boardman, married Nathaniel Bowditch, a Federalist, in 1798, but died later that year. Bowditch then married his cousin Mary Ingersoll (MoBrDa), whose mother was Mary Hodges, a cousin of Elizabeth's mother (FaBrDa) with the same name. The situation is complicated further in that Elizabeth's cousin (MoBrDa) was married to William Silsbee, the brother of Senator Nathaniel Silsbee. Benjamin Hodges (William Silsbee's father-in-law and Mary Boardman's brother) seems to be a key member of the Hodges family, tying together the Silsbees, Boardmans, Hodgeses, and Crowninshields; indications from Bentley's diary are that Benjamin Hodges, unlike other Hodges relatives, was a Republican (EIHC 1882, p. 292). The Crowninshield genealogy is complicated further by the marriage of John (brother of Benjamin W., Jacob, and Mary Silsbee) to his cousin Maria Crowninshield (FaBrDa), and the marriage of the brother Jacob to his cousin Sarah Gardner (MoSiDa). The pattern of marital alliances among the Crowninshields, Boardmans, Hodges, and Silsbees, indicates that networks of marital alliances occurred among Republicans as well as Federalists.

Figure 4-1
Crowninshield-Derby-Silsbee-Boardman-Hodges Intermarriages

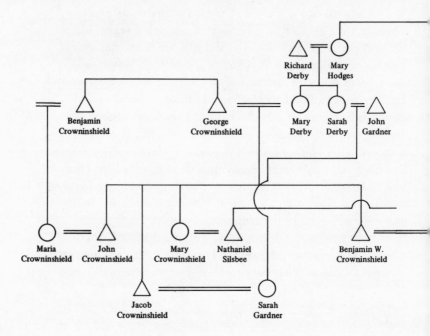

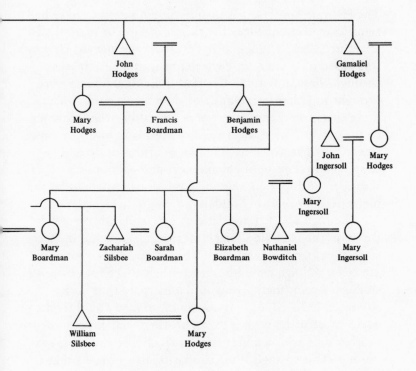

First-Cousin Marriage

The Hebraic family-organization model seems to have had significant consequences for the formation of marital alliances in Salem. The social structure of the ancient Hebrews was based on a close tie between related males. It was through these masculine ties that individual houses were brought together into clans and then into a nation. The more ties in existence, the greater would be the solidarity of the group. There was thus an impetus to multiply these ties as much as possible. Familial relationships could be supplemented by political alliances and economic partnerships. In kinship, consanguineal relationships could be supplemented by marital bonds.

The high sex differentiation and strong sibling solidarity in the Hebraic social structure suggest that in Salem society, which followed the Hebraic model, ties between same-sex siblings would be firmer than those for cross-sex siblings. Accordingly, we would anticipate that in the Salem of 1770-1820, first-cousin marriages would tend to occur more often with father's brother's daughter and with mother's sister's daughter than with children of cross-sex siblings. This strong sibling solidarity also suggests that a major way for exchange to occur between families would be for the two sets of siblings to intermarry with one another. In that manner, alliances could be maintained from one generation to the next with multiple family ties. Thus we would anticipate that not only would marriage between parallel cousins tend to occur but also marriages denoting sibling-exchange.

Despite the relative infrequency of first-cousin marriages, the study of marriages between siblings' children

seems significant for understanding how the family is related
to political and economic institutions in the community.
In addition, first-cousin marriages may suggest the character of husband-wife relationships.

In relating first-cousin marriage to social structure, it is
important to note whether a man marries his cousin on the
mother's side or the father's side. The uncle or aunt who
provides him with a wife apparently maintains a close tie
with his parents. In a society where male kinship ties are
emphasized, if the children of two sisters marry, they are
in effect tying together the previously unrelated families of
the sisters' husbands. Such an arrangement would denote
the creation of unstable alliances, which might not persist
through future generations. On the other hand, if the children of two brothers married, the marriage would merely
multiply previously existing male bonds to perpetuate and
strengthen an existing alliance.

The genealogies of families appearing in Bentley's 1790
list, as well as the family histories in the *Essex Institute
Historical Collections* (especially volumes 1-27), were care-
fully scanned for first-cousin marriages. Particular attention was paid to the maiden names of the mothers of
husbands and wives. In a marriage with father's sister's
daughter, the husband's last name is the same as his wife's
maiden name. Where a man marries his mother's brother's
daughter, his wife's and mother's maiden name are the
same. The most difficult situation for tracing first-cousin
marriages is obviously one in which a man marries his
mother's sister's daughter; here care must be taken to
determine whether the husband's mother and his wife's
mother had the same maiden name. The clues offered by
these maiden names of mothers in first-cousin marriage
must then be investigated to determine whether in fact the
parents of the two spouses were siblings. In most cases,

having the same name actually denoted a more distant relationship, and it indicated that many of the marriages in the vicinity of Salem took place between second cousins or more distant relatives. The work of scanning, however, was eased somewhat by the propensity of genealogists to be attentive to first-cousin marriages. Often they indicated that the marriage had taken place between cousins, although they seldom traced the exact relationships. Sometimes what was called a cousin marriage in the genealogy turned out to be one between second cousins.

The analysis of first-cousin marriages was restricted in several ways. First, it included only those marriages in which the evidence that the parents were siblings was explicit in the genealogy. Second, the timespan covered was confined to a half-century between 1770 and 1820. A shorter timespan would have yielded too few cases; a longer one would have meant including marriages occurring long before the American Revolution and after the Industrial Revolution. Third, the small number of first-cousin marriages necessitated the inclusion of families living outside Salem but in its vicinity (such as in Marblehead, Danvers, Lynn, Topsfield, and other communities in Essex County). Occasionally, when families migrated from Salem to Boston, the marriages of their children in Boston were included in the analysis.

In all, forty-two first-cousin marriages were found which conformed to the criteria listed in the previous paragraph. There were a few marriages between even closer relatives. (For example, Thomas Ashby married his brother's daughter Esther Ashby.) And instances occurred of stepbrothers marrying their stepsisters (Oliver Pope and Mary Fabens; James Perkins and Hannah Kinsman). In one family, Bentley (1905, I, p. 366) reports: "The Children are of three sorts, & are intermarrying, as the present is a

* * *

Family, Politics, and Marital Alliances

third wife, & the wives had children by other husbands."
Marrying relatives across generations was not unusual: John
Babbige and Sarah Becket (MoBrSoDa), John Ropes and
Abigail Ropes (FaFaBrSoSoDa), or John Titcomb Ropes
and Jane Ropes (FaFaFaBrSoSoSoDa).

The previous chapter on the family and economic relationships suggested that relationships between brothers
might vary at different socioeconomic levels. Accordingly,
separate analyses were performed for families at high and
middle levels. There were no first-cousin marriages uncov-
ered among families in which most men were laborers,
fishermen, or mariners. Extended families at high socioeconomic levels were those in which the men were mainly
merchants, professionals, or sea captains. The middle-SES
extended families had men who were artisans of one kind
or another. Of course, branches within the high and middle
level categories departed in socioeconomic characteristics
from the general level; when this occurred, the deviant
branch was treated separately in the analysis.

The distribution of first-cousin marriages by the husband's consanguineal relationship to his wife is indicated in
Table 4-1. This table compares the distribution for high
and middle SES. The major differences between the two
groups are found in the categories father's brother's daughter and mother's sister's daughter. The middle-SES couples
tend to be concentrated in the father's brother's daughter's
category, while the high SES couples tend to fall into the
mother's sister's daughter's category. (Although random
sampling was not used, a Chi square test was computed
and was significant at the .05 level. Chi square = 6.44; 2 d.f.)

Table 4-2 indicates more clearly the ways in which
cousin marriages differ in high and in middle socioeco-
nomic-status families. First-cousin marriages among high
SES families tended to occur between parallel cousins

* * *

Guardians of Virtue

Table 4-1
Cousin Marriages in Salem Area

Wife's Relationship to Husband	Socioeconomic Status		
	High	Middle	Total
FaBrDa	7	9	16
Cross-Cousin (MoBrDa or FaSiDa)	8	7	15
MoSiDa	10	1	11
Total	25	17	42

(a man and his FaBrDa or MoSiDa), with the degree of association Kendall's Q = .65. The importance of uncles in the middle-SES group is suggested by the finding that 14 of the 17 cousin marriages in middle-SES families occured with father's *brother's* daughter or mother's *brother's* daughter.

Table 4-2
First-Cousin Marriages in Salem Area
(by specific relationship)

Blood Relationship of Parent-in-Law to Husband	High SES*			Middle SES		
	Wife From:			Wife From:		
	Father's Side	Mother's Side	Total	Father's Side	Mother's Side	Total
Uncle	7	5	12	9	5	14
Aunt	3	10	13	2	1	3
	10	15	25	11	6	17

*High SES: Kendall's Q = .65.

*   *   *

Family, Politics, and Marital Alliances

Although the number of first-cousin marriages was small, cousin pairings did not seem to occur in a haphazard fashion. Among families at high socioeconomic levels, there were 25 first-cousin marriages which could have involved 50 different last names. However, six extended families contributed more than half of the participants in these marriages: Nichols (seven), Cabot (five, in addition to Cabot as a middle name), Ropes (five), and the Crownin-shields, Peirces, and Sparhawks (three each). The multiple ties created by the first-cousin marriages in these families thus do not seem to have occurred by chance marital selection.

Another form of marriage which reinforced ties between families also occurred in the Salem area from 1770 to 1820. In 27 instances, sibling sets exchanged brothers and sisters. (There were numerous other instances when the same last name occurred among two or more spouses of siblings; however, the data were insufficient to determine whether these spouses were actually siblings.) In thirteen cases, the brother-sister exchange was symmet-rical, with a man marrying the sister of his own sister's hus-band. Thirteen other exchanges were asymmetrical, with brothers in one family marrying sisters in another. There was also one case in which three sibling marriages occurred, with two brothers and a sister in one family and two sisters and a brother in the other.

The occurrence of sibling exchange seems to be related to the practice of first-cousin marriage among high-socio-economic-status families. Like cousin marriage, marriage between sets of siblings appears to be associated especially with the creation of alliances between politically active and powerful families. This tendency can be illustrated by the Sparhawk-King and the Higginson-Cabot intermarriages shown in Figures 4-2 and 4-3. In these figures, only those siblings involved in marriages with relatives are shown. Including siblings who have married outside the families, would have so complicated the charts that their usefulness in illustrating bonds created by first-cousin marriage and sibling intermarriage would have been dissipated.

The Sparhawk family, described earlier in the chapter, had been politically strong prior to the Revolution and maintained close ties with English branches afterwards. They were wealthy and anti-Republican. As indicated in Figure 4-2 there was a history of first-cousin marriage within the family, with Nathaniel Sparhawk marrying his father's brother's daughter Kathryn Sparhawk. Just prior to the Revolution, Kathryn's brother John married Abigail King, and Abigail's brother George, in turn, married John's sister Susannah. The other King sister, Mary, married a Daniel Humphreys. In the following generation, after the Revolution, the Sparhawk, King, and Humphreys bonds were reinforced through the first-cousin marriages of the junior Daniel Humphreys with Kathryn Sparhawk and of George King Sparhawk with A. Humphreys, both marriages occurring in 1794. The Sparhawk-King-Humphreys intermarriages indicate how the combination of first-cousin marriage and sibling-exchange tends to perpetuate a self-contained kinship-group, even in a bilaterial kinship system. In this case, the sibling-exchange was symmetrical, and both kinds of parallel cousin-marriage (FaBrDa and MoSiDa) were present.

The various first-cousin and sibling-exchange marriages in the Cabot family are shown in Figure 4-3. John Cabot came from the Isle of Jersey in 1742 and married an Orne. A number of marriages took place between Cabot descendents and the Ornes; the precise relationships, however, are difficult to trace. In the mid-eighteenth century, there was considerable sibling exchange between the second-

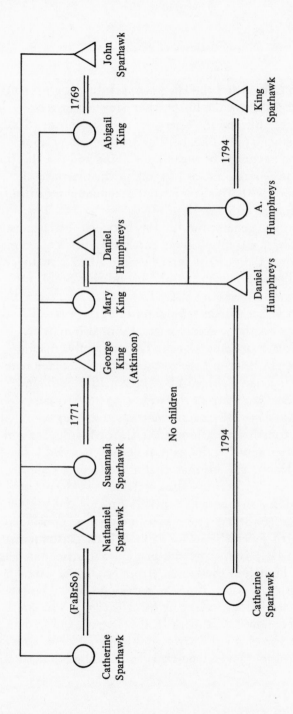

Figure 4-2

Sparhawk Family: Cousin-Marriages and Sibling-Exchanges

generation Cabots and the Higginsons. John Higginson married Esther Cabot, while his brother Steven married Esther's sister Elizabeth. A sister of the Higginsons (Sarah) married Esther's (and Elizabeth's) brother John Cabot. Finally, the exchange between the Cabots and the Higginsons of that generation was capped by the marriage of Joseph Cabot with his sister Esther's stepdaughter Elizabeth Higginson.

In the third generation, the ties between the Higginsons and the Cabots were multiplied further by first-cousin marriages. George Cabot (who later became a U.S. Senator) married Elizabeth Higginson, and his brother Stephen Cabot married Elizabeth's sister Deborah. These were marriages with father's sister's daughter in both instances. Two other Cabot brothers, Andrew and John, also married sisters, this time members of the Dodge family. Also in this generation, Joseph Lee, whose mother's maiden name was Orne, married George Cabot's sister Elizabeth, and when she died, he married the widow of her brother Stephen (Deborah Higginson, mentioned above).

In the fourth generation of the Cabot family, the son of Elizabeth Cabot (Nathaniel Cabot Lee) married Mary Ann, the daughter of his maternal uncle George Cabot. At the same time, Frederick Cabot and another Mary Ann Cabot, children of George's brothers Francis and Samuel, also married (FaBrDa). (First-cousin marriages continued into the fifth generation, with Francis J. Higginson marrying his FaSiDa.) There was also brother-and-sister exchange in the Lee branch of the family (from Nathaniel Cabot Lee above), with one sister, Amelia, marrying Charles Jackson and a brother, Henry, marrying Mary Jackson. The cousins of the Lee children, Elizabeth, Sally (Susan), and Lydia, married the brothers of Charles and Mary Jackson. One Jackson brother (James) married first Elizabeth and then, after her death, her sister Sally. The intermarriages are complicated further by the marriage of Charles Jackson (later a Supreme Court Justice of Massachusetts) with Fanny Cabot after the death of his first wife, Amelia Lee. Other Dodge and Orne descendants are spotted throughout the genealogy; however, the data are too inadequate to indicate the nature of these relationships.

Like the Sparhawks, the Cabots are thus characterized by numerous instances of sibling-exchange and first-cousin marriages. However, the sibling-exchange marriages among the Cabots seem to be much more complex than those among the Sparhawks and thereby create more numerous bonds between families. Moreover, whereas the Sparhawks' first-cousin marriages were between parallel cousins, those of the Cabots include cross-cousins as well. In both the Sparhawk and Cabot genealogies, however, the kinds of cousin-marriages seemed to alternate from one generation to the next: whereas the parental generation married cousins on the father's side, their children married the mother's relatives. (See Lamb, 1952, p. 118, for Cabot-Lowell marriages.)

The rapidly changing political and economic situation in the United States during the period of 1790-1810 caused many shifting alliances. Unlike a nation whose government is based on a stable landed aristocracy, the American government was influenced by the vacillation in political and economic power of the Federalists and the Republicans. Coupled with the system of succession whereby inheritance is shared, the republican form of government seems to have inhibited the development of a consistent form of cross-cousin marriage (e.g., MoBrDa) among the wealthy. A consistent form of cousin-marriage, evolving into a tradition, might have created a single dominating class, such as the Chin society described by Lehman (1963). Instead, the

Figure 4-3
Higginson and Cabot Families: Cousin-Marriages and Sibling Exchanges

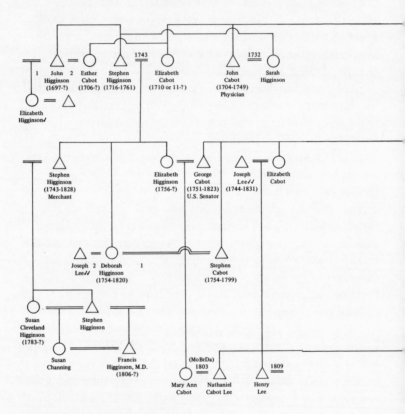

✓ Elizabeth Higginson married FaBrWiBr (also FaWi, Br)
✓✓ Joseph Lee married: 1st Elizabeth Cabot; 2nd Deborah Higginson

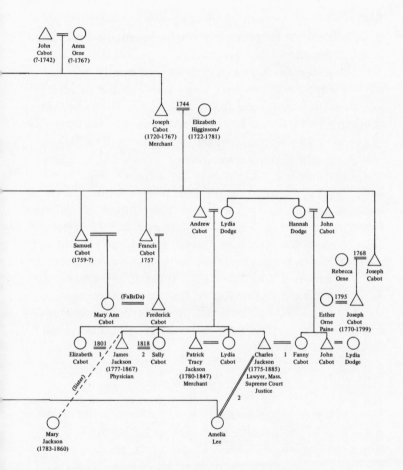

high-SES marital alliances through sibling-exchange and diverse forms of first-cousin marriage seemed better suited to the formation and maintenance of political factions.

The previous chapter suggested that family ties between male relatives were more stable in the middle, artisan class than they were in the higher merchant class. That tendency is borne out by the predominance of artisan marriages with an uncle's daughter (particularly FaBrDa), which cemented ties between the brothers and between uncle and nephew. Cohesion in the artisan families was based less on the need for political and economic alliances and more on mutual aid and apprenticeship with relatives. Cousin-marriages in the artisan class proved more effective than those in the merchant class in producing kinship solidarity. Consequently, conjugal units in the merchant class would be more autonomous than those in the artisan class. Although the actual number of first-cousin marriages was small in the 1770-1820 period, the forms which cousin-marriage took seem to have reflected in American social structure of that time.

Lower-Class Marriage

Lower-class marriage seems to have differed markedly from that in other socioeconomic segments in Salem. This section sketches the character of marriage in relation to various aspects of lower-class married life, especially its precariousness. In doing so, the discussion focuses on such phenomena as matrifocality, divorce, and desertion.

The contrast between lower-class marriage and marriage at other socioeconomic levels is suggested by data on the relative degree of remarriage among occupational classes. Table 4-3 shows the percentages of men and women who had more than one marriage. The data are for men married

* * *

Family, Politics, and Marital Alliances

for the first time between 1751 and 1805 (and their first wives). These men were relatives of members of the East Church in 1790, listed in the Bentley diary.

According to Table 4-3, approximately one-third of the merchants married more than once. Generally, the merchants did not take castoff, experienced widows who might dominate them in either their first or subsequent marriages. Instead they tended to take young brides who were marrying for the first time. This tendency may have facilitated patriarchal inclinations in the merchant class as contrasted with proneness to matriarchy in the laboring class.[2]

Table 4-3 also indicates that, compared with men of higher socioeconomic levels, laboring-class men seldom had more than one marriage; this situation may be attributed in part to their low median age at death. Yet even when they survived their wives, they presumably had some difficulty in procuring new wives. About one-third of the laboring-class women, however, who often outlived their husbands by 15-20 years (median: 18 years), married at least once again. Since most Salem marriages took place within socioeconomic classes, probably laborers, mariners, and fishermen were more likely to marry widows than were members of other occupational classes. From the lower-class woman's viewpoint, widowhood may have precluded upward mobility through marriage. (Percentages for persons in the occupation unknown category resemble those for the laboring class; it is likely that many of these couples were also in the laborer-mariner-fishermen occupational category.)

The marital life of the lower-class population in Salem

[2] The total amount of remarriage (15 percent) is below that found by Demos (1970) for Plymouth and may itself reflect the decline of the prescription of living under strong family government.

is difficult to describe in detail because of the paucity of data. Various sources, such as the *Salem Vital Records*, Bentley's *Diary*, Perley's *History of Salem, Massachusetts*, and the *Essex Institute Historical Collections*, must be scanned to obtain even a sketchy outline of lower-class family life.

Table 4-3
Percentage of Persons Married More Than Once, for Men First Married in 1751-1805 and Their First Wives
(by occupational class of husband)

Occupational Class	Men in More Than One Marriage		Women in More Than One Marriage		Total Number of Men or Women Married at Least Once
	N	Per Cent	N	Per Cent	
Merchants and Professionals	26	31.3	4	4.8	83
Sea Captains	21	15.8	16	12.0	133
Artisans	28	21.7	12	9.3	129
Laborers, Mariners, and Fishermen	8	9.0	28	31.1	90*
Occupation Unknown	4	3.6	30	27.3	110
Total	89	13.8	90	14.0	645*

*The number of times one of the laborers had been married was unknown; the total for men in that category therefore was 89, and the total for women 90. Similarly, the overall percentages are based on 644 men and 645 women. Based on relatives of members of the East Church of Salem in 1790 listed in the Bentley diary.

The piecing together of the events in the family life of Benjamin Nourse, listed in the 1790 census as a baker, indicates the inferences required to present a picture of a lower-class marriage. His date of birth is unknown. His wife Margaret Welcome was born in 1748 and was baptized as an Episcopalian in 1758. Benjamin and Margaret married in 1774. According to Perley, they had four children: (1) Margaret, born about 1784; (2) Edward, born in 1785 and died on October 28, 1786; (3) John, born about 1788 and died July 10, 1791; and (4) John, baptized June 5, 1791. The *Vital Records* indicate that another daughter Margaret died at 14 months on August 24, 1778. Of the surviving children, Margaret and John, only Margaret is known to have lived to adulthood.

A major event which apparently affected the Nourse family's destiny was the death of Mrs. Nourse's brother Thomas Welcome, a baker. Thomas was evidently the proprietor of the bakery in which Benjamin Nourse worked. Benjamin Nourse was listed as a baker in the records through 1790. However, on January 10, 1791, Thomas Welcome's estate was sold, and afterwards, as in 1792, Benjamin was listed as a laborer. Since the occupation of baker seems to have had the connotation of a somewhat higher socioeconomic status than that of laborer, very likely the Nourse family suffered financially and socially following the brother-in-law's death. The effect on Benjamin must have been profound; on November 18, 1792, Bentley reports in his diary that he visited or prayed for Margaret Nourse and her children for "husband deprived of his reason." The next entry made by Bentley for the Nourse family is for June 7, 1795, when he reports that he has consoled Margaret Nourse for her husband who is near death. The only other reference made by Bentley to the Nourse family is in 1815, when he consoled the sister of Mrs. Nourse over the latter's death.

The downfall of the Nourse family is indicated further

in the *Vital Records*. An entry for September 1, 1811, indicates that Margaret, the daughter of Margaret and Benjamin Nourse, died of a complication of ills at the age of 27. Margaret was unmarried, brought from Boston, and died at the poorhouse.

The end of the Nourse family came on November 7, 1815 with the death of Margaret, Benjamin's widow, who died according to the *Vital Records* at the age of 67 at the charity house. The *Vital Records* indicates only that she married at the age of 26 and lived 30 years in married life. That final notation raises the question as to whether Benjamin died in 1795 or in 1804. Benjamin's fate will probably never be known. In all likelihood, however, it was an unhappy one.

The brief outline of the Nourse family history indicates also the extent to which fortuitous circumstances played an important part in the lives of the Salem poor. Causes of death of the Nourses included cough and convulsions, "bloody flux," fever, and a complication of ills— all of which may be related to living in poverty. Moreover, had Mrs. Nourse's brother, Thomas Welcome, not died, the Nourse family might have lived in more comfortable circumstances. As it was, Thomas Welcome's widow had to support herself as a shopkeeper in order to remain alive. In Salem in the 1790s, widowed shopkeepers apparently eked out a bare existence (since their male children were generally bound out as apprentices, as in other poor families). Although the Nourse ancestors appeared in Salem in 1640, the family had always been poor, and relatives seem to have offered little assistance to ease the plight of Benjamin and Margaret Nourse and their children in the 1790-1815 period.

There is little doubt about the misery and precariousness of lower-class life in Salem and in the surrounding communities. A traveler in Essex County commented on the poverty-stricken in Marblehead:

> October 23, 1775. . . . We pass'd on over a Stony Road to Marblehead which is a dirty disagreeable Place at present they are here in great Distress as the Town is built amongst Rocks & Stones, where is no land to cultivate.
>
> Marblehead and the people in general are Fishermen or concern'd in that Way, which Source of Support is now at an end many of the men are in the army & the Rest are out of Employ and almost every house swarms with Children of these hardy, temporate Men—
>
> Their situation is miserable the Streets & Road are fill'd [with] the poor little Boys & Girls who are forc'd beg of all they see the Women are lazy & of Consequence dirty Creatures. [EIHC, 1947, pp. 144-145]

Generally, as it might be anticipated, the poor met with little compassion among the élite. Instead, the élite feared them, although their alcoholic intemperance was preferable to riot and revolt. Bentley writes:

> October 28, 1790. In conversation with a Gentleman of property upon his motives for a removal to Boston, he observed that the internal police of the town was in such hands as to render it a disgrace & an injury to be an inhabitant. . . . Last evening shared in the disgust arising from opposing the conversation current among the people of undervaluing all the institutions of civil society.
>
> April 16, 1791. . . . A Question whether intemperance [is] more common now, than formerly. Facts are that rude insults to signposts, poles, & houses are confessed to be less frequent. But it is replied that the absence from Public worship gives an opportunity of practicing more securely, & the many purchases of Rum on Sunday attest the fact. Besides the labourers are more addicted to daily excess, tho' not to riots as before.

> Aug. 23, 1791. . . . Noise enough has been made that our streets were full of beggars, not of our own growth. The streets have been cleared, & to keep them so, the Cage has been invented. The complaint is now charged against the Officers of the Town for doing their duty.

These comments reveal the conditions with which Salem's powerless lower class had to cope in order to survive. They express the resentment by the laboring class of the élite. The Federalist self-conception as the party of "law and order" probably occurred as a reaction to the laboring class's resorting to riot, "rude insult" to property and person, and escape into intemperance.

The position of families in the political structure of Salem was mirrored in the marital relationships. Unlike the strong marital alliances in the merchant and artisan classes, the marital bonds of families at the unskilled occupational levels were weak. Although the extent of marital disruptions and the degree of matrifocality in family organization are difficult to estimate because of the poor quality of data pertaining to lower-class families, reports in the historical collections and in the Bentley diary suggest a high frequency of marital breakups.

Matrifocality

The presence of matrifocal families in Salem is evident in the Bentley diary. In matrifocal families, a woman and her children form a stable residential group without the regular presence of a husband-father, and they maintain an enduring relationship with the woman's consanguineal kin. According to an analysis by Kunstadter (1963), matrifocality tends to occur where the division of labor separates adult males and females, and the sex ratio is unbalanced, with a surplus of women.

* * *

Family, Politics, and Marital Alliances

Table 4-4
Population of Salem in 1800
(sex ratios by age)*

Age Categories	Free White Males	Free White Females	Total	Sex Ratio
Under 10 years of age	1,278	1,244	1,522	103
Of 10 and under 16	745	758	1,503	98
Of 16 and under 26, including heads of families	950	1,094	2,044	87
Of 26 and under 45, including heads of families	901	1,041	1,942	87
Of 45 and upwards, including heads of families	433	705	1,138	61
All other free persons, except Indians not taxed			308	
Total			9,457	

*U.S. Census, 1801, p. 8. Age categories from census report.

Both of these conditions existed in lower-class Salem.
The men either went to sea or were often forced to seek
work outside of Salem. They sometimes migrated or
deserted their families, so that male absence in the lower
class was common. Like the division of labor, the sex ratio
in Salem also favored the development of matrifocality in
family organization. The Salem sex ratio in 1800 is shown
in Table 4-4. According to the table, although the sex ratio
for children under 16 hovered around 100, there was an
excess of adult females. For young adults in the child-

bearing years, ages 16-44, the sex ratio was about 87. For older persons it declined markedly: the sex ratio for persons 45 and over was 61. Hence, both the male-female separation and the sex ratio facilitated the sprouting of matrifocal families.

Although data are insufficient to permit an estimate of number of matrifocal family groups in Salem and in the surrounding communities, apparently matrifocality was fairly widespread. According to Bentley:

> February 16, 1790. . . . In the [Salem] Gazette they represent that there are now living [in Marblehead, just outside of Salem] "no less than four hundred & fifty-nine widows, and eight hundred & sixty-five Orphans, five hundred of which are Females." Some of them may however be Widows like the woman of Samaria.[3] The number of Widows is not a third more than in Salem, & the children not being two to a mother, & about one daughter, nothing but a characteristic want of economy, even in the worst state of the fishery can be the cause of suffering.

Bentley's view of the immorality of these families is revealed in his entries regarding the Burke family:

> March 23, 1791. Mercy Burke's child's dead. Her G. Mother & Mother lived together in a miserable hovel, with 4 others miserable by the lowest vices, & in extreme poverty.
> May 2, 1791. The overseer . . . ordered into confinement the infamous family named Burke's, alias White's, alias Masury. The G. G. Mother, & G. Mother, Mother & children, who long near the Neckgate have been infamous for all the vices.

---

[3] (John 4) "She answered, 'I have no husband.' 'You are right,' said Jesus, 'in saying that you have no husband, for although you have had five husbands, the man with whom you are now living is not your husband.' " [The New English Bible, New Testament]

> May 14, 1791. . . . The woman, named Burke, alias
> White, alias Masury, that has had so many notes at the
> meeting, & was carried last Monday week into the charity
> house, died last Tuesday from ulcers in the Lungs. The
> public satisfaction in an event was never more clearly
> expressed, from the abhorrence of her vices. This single
> death separates the whole family, & may afford room for
> the timely reformation of the children.

However, Bentley's tendency to attribute matrifocality
to immoral impulses was lessened by the fact that women
in these families were not uniformly consistent in their
"addiction to low vices." Like others in Salem, they were
complex persons, and sometimes Bentley had to explain
their deviance in terms of different forces. He thus recognized another class of motivation, wherein deviance was
ascribed to the inability to control impulses—constitu-
tional errors, the force of natural propensity, high passions.
These are illustrated in three Bentley entries:

> May 1, 1791. . . . The Children christened this day were
> begotten by several Fathers, but born of one mother, whose
> continence is surprising, excepting in this single respect. She
> is exemplary for her neatness, prudence, & love of her chil-
> dren. She is a proof that there may be a constitutional error,
> & that this propensity may not involve the low Vices.
> January 30, 1790. This day a woman by the name of
> Welch was delivered of Twins in the South fields & died after
> delivery. One child has survived her. This is the fourth time
> of bearing Twins, & the woman is now possessed of no law-
> ful husband, & 46 years of age wt 300 lb. The force of natural
> propensity is strikingly seen, & why may not the natural child
> verify the old observation respecting genius, *got by lustful
> stealth of nature.*
> January 23, 1799. A request having been repeated, sent
> from Anna Wyatt now at Andover, . . . that I would . . . call

upon her before her death. . . . The cause of her request was a
desire to secure to her natural children, what the Law unjustly
deprives them of, such property as she was in possession of at
her decease. The history of this young woman is—She was
born of parents who lived at variance, & the father, in the
coasting trade, for many years made his home in the sloop at
the wharf when in port. The children were all of warm tem-
pers & greatly at variance. This d. being the youngest child,
lived with the mother & yet had all the affections of the
father & by her was the only communication between all
things between the parents. In all other points but that of
domestic variance, the parents were unexceptionable. . . .
Everywhere her company was desired. And when the sons
of God came together Satan came also among them. A
young man named Bray, of good person, paid her every
attention & seduced & then abandoned her. She had refused
the addresses of a young man of greater industry, but less
address, who had succeeded well in the world. In this situation she was forsaken by all her young companions & was
without the resources of good counsel, which may relieve
the misery of such conditions. She fell sick & was for long
time very low but recovered. After several years she was
addressed by a young carpenter, a stranger & widower. He
at length seduced her, lived with her, encouraging her hopes,
till his debauchery and abuse obliged her & all her friends to
call upon the police & expose her to the public notice. She
was confined in the public workhouse till he would consent
to leave the Town, & she, infeebled by the worse abuse which
ever was known, retired to Andover to finish a life that
opened with the best prospects & closed at 33 years of age
with the worst. No vice was to be charged to her but high
passions. She had retained her patrimony which, in the best
manner she could, she bequeathed to her two natural daughters, which Charity of the noblest kind has in charge.

The biological explanation provided the inhabitants of
Salem with a way of handling marked deviance from the

Puritanical model of family organization in cases where women conformed in most respects to the ethical code. Without that alternative explanation, the impoverished state of the otherwise moral women in matrifocal families could not be justified. These cases were regarded as exceptions to the relationship between deviant family organization and immorality.

Divorce

Like matrifocality, divorce in the lower class also was justified on the basis of two alternative explanations: immorality and incompatibility. Incompatibility, as a natural occurrence, did not imply damnation. Since most lower-class divorces did not receive legal sanction, the frequency of divorce cannot be estimated. In general, the family was still regarded as the basic social unit in Salem society, and domestic decisions (including divorce and separation) remained in the sphere of family government. Legal action was probably taken when much property was involved, and/or no settlement could be reached within the family. When property disposition was involved, divorce became a public matter, as indicated by the publication of notices in newspapers. Although most of these notices stated merely the refusal by the husband to be accountable for his wife's debts, occasionally they also announced the termination of the marital relationship. The paid advertisement by Thomas Stevens in the *Salem Gazette* of January 12, 1790, read:

> Whereas Elizabeth, my wife, has become an intemperate, quarrelsome, and troublesome woman, inasmuch that it is impossible to live with her in peace and decency, I am therefore determined not to cohabit with her any longer, while she continues her present evil courses; this is therefore to caution all

persons against trusting her on my account, as I declared I will
not pay any debt of her contrakting, to the smallest amot.

Sometimes, however, a property settlement could be
reached, and the marriage would likely be terminated by a
private contract. When Timothy Dexter, a speculator who
was suddenly catapulted into wealth, divorced his wife,
he did so by private contract. Bentley noted in his diary:

> September 6, 1792. Timothy [Dexter of Newburyport] has
> now parted from his wife because she is old, upon a contract
> paid of 2,000 £ & the horse and chaise, & is looking out for
> a young wife.

Apparently the divorce case of Nathaniel and Margaret
Derby West would not have come to court if the parties
had been able to settle their property arrangements by
themselves. According to Bentley:

> Nov. 8, 1806. It is announced that the case of West & West is
> to come in on Tuesday if not settled by the parties. He is a
> Son of an honest Citizen & Master of a Vessel, & She the
> eldest daughter of the late E. H. Derby. She fell in love with
> this man wonderfully, & has now as wonderfully eloped, &
> sued for a divorce. The weakness, to say nothing else betrayed
> on the occasion, is indeed without a parallel in my times. The
> public know not which to give pity or contempt.
> Nov. 11, 1806. . . . Contrary to the will of her father &
> friends [she] persisted in marrying West. Never could John-
> son's words better [be] applied, when a man married a for-
> tune it is not all he marries. The woman became all that is
> execrable in women from vanity, caprice, folly, & malignity
> & after every quarrel with all her relatives she waged open
> war against her husband & this day, aided by the unfeeling
> perseverance of her malignant Br[other] Gen. E. H. D[erby]

who has a private quarrel to avenge, she displayed in open
court, to prove the incontinency of Capt. W[est], all the
sweepings of the Brothels of Boston, & all the vile wretches
of Salem, Marblehead, Cape Ann, &c. &c. The concourse on
the occasion was immense & the alarm great, as no person
can be safe in his reputation after such proceedings.

Nov. 13, 1806. This day the pleas on the case of West &
West were in the S[upreme] J[udicial] Court. . . . [The
judges] dined this day with Gen. Derby who conducted the
persecution & left no doubt that they had formed a judgment at the expence of Capt. West. The public indignation
was roused but the Judges are the Jury.

Nov. 14, 1806. The Courts determined the Divorce. . . .
It is some relief in reflecting on these transactions that all
concerned are in the opposition & that no republican is concerned even as a constable.

Nov. 15, 1806. The affair of the Divorce still depending
& it is said has been concluded by consent of parties. The
wife is to have the farm in Danvers & real estate as it is & 3
thousand dollars a year, with trustees for the principal, and
the trustees named are the Brother John D[erby] & the
Brother in Law B. Pickman. . . . Gen. D[erby] has contrived
a law & aided a malicious prosecution to gratify his enmity
to West & to possess & injure his property.

In contrast to the scandal and notoriety associated with
the West divorce case, divorce in the lower class was
accepted as a normal course of events. As indicated earlier,
divorce was interpreted either in terms of the immorality
of the partners, which reaffirmed personal commitments
to the traditional family values for the rest of the community, or in terms of incompatibility, which was deemed a
reasonable basis for marital breakup. One could excuse the
pious in this situation. Divorce was not in itself a reason to
condemn the partners. Several examples are presented
from the Bentley diary:

March 17, 1809. Buried this day Elizabeth Waters, aet. 27, d[aughter] of my old friend Capt. John Becket. She married a worthless young man of whom the world had good hopes & who had ample means of being happy. A Seperation [sic] by the consent of all the friends on both sides ensued & he withdrew from the town. She lingered in consumption & died.
    Nov. 24, 1811. . . . The daughters [of Joseph Franks, a laborer] married miserably, but are free of their husbands by consent, & one is with the parents & the other in a house belonging to him.
    Nov. 8, 1812. At the Court this sitting at Salem were two divorces obtained. One of . . . a son of General Foster, now in prison & who has been in the penitentiary, from his wife, daughter of Pierce of Salem. The very bad habits of this young man, & the good hopes of his wife justify this lenity of the law.

Desertion

    The uncertainty of marital bonds among the lower class in Salem is probably best reflected in desertion. Like matrifocality and divorce, the frequency of desertions by husbands in Salem is difficult to estimate. The lower-class occupations often required absence from home: mariners and fishermen might go on long journeys, and laborers might seek work in other communities. Consequently, sometimes it is difficult to determine whether an absence should be construed as desertion or not. Bentley notes:

July 14, 1791. After all our fears Capt. Chipman arrived this day from Trinidada, to our no small pleasure. The fears . . . respecting absent heads of families, &c.
    Oct. 14, 1790. . . . In the war, being absent, his wife tho' with a numerous family married a stranger, & upon her husband's return refused to renew her former connections, & moved away with her new husband & children from the State. Lander since married a Country girl, & has one child.

Salem Vital Records also indicates:

April 7, 1802. Death of Hannah, wife of James Murray
[a mariner] Consumption, 33, married at 20. Left one child,
a dau. Her husband has not been heard of for several years.
She . . . has lost two children this year. [EIHC, 16, p. 29]
    July 29, 1815. George, child of George & Mary Wright.
Mortification of bowels, 4 months. Fine child, good mother.
Complaint not well understood. . . . Mother a Scot. Father
from Gothenburg in Sweden. Has been long absent at sea.
One child, a son left. [EIHC, 19, p. 30]

For the most part, however, desertion was regarded as
immoral. Entries in Bentley's diary include:

December 14, 1794—Sunday. There was something singular
on the notes this day. All the cases were of separation. The
Widow Bowditch was left by her husband many years since.
Capt. William Wyatt who died at New Orleans, left his family
several years since. The Father does not visit or cohabit with
his wife. Mrs. Martin who died in the Charity house was left
by her husband, who may be yet living, as far as we know.
    May 22, 1794. The Mr. Eulin [a mariner] who married
into the White family, & against whom so many exertions
were made, has already proved his business by leaving his
wife, carrying off all her property he could command,
embezzling cash paid to him to discharge debts, & as the last
consolation he has written to her, that he was but an old
man, & that if she was uneasy at his long absence, she might
easily call in her neighbors.
    July 20, 1790. Attended the Baptism of a Mary Whitte-
more. Her father has absented from his family, & has become
wretched by his vices. The Mother lived in the New Fort, &
then removed into the Upper part of the Town. She has since
returned among us into Uncle Diman's House, for the Bene-
fit of a Son in the Ropewalk. The young woman is in a
declining state.

The Bentley diary also portrays men who have sought work elsewhere, partly to avoid interacting with their wives. The issue of evil is clouded even further by entries in which Bentley describes men and women living together, unmarried but industrious and temperate:

> March 6, 1814. Sunday. Richard Palfrey & wife & children, p. death of his daughter Eliza, aet. 22. . . . This man has lived in a singular manner. He has property, industry, & temperance but he lives with a women [sic] he has never married, & his children appear to have had no just share of his affection. He provides food abundantly but no cloathing or other accommodations suited to his condition. A very singular case.

Summary: Marital Instability in the Lower Class

In brief, the pooling of personal and financial resources through the creation of marital and business alliances permitted the merchant and artisan families to compensate for the uncertainties of life. These alliances enabled the families involved to maintain some semblance of control over their existence. However, the lower-class families could not muster resources to dissipate uncertainty by forming such alliances. Instead, marital stability was precarious, and laboring-class families were left without political and economic power in the community.

Conclusion: Power and Partisanship

Marriage was utilized differently in the various strata of Salem society. In the merchant class, families formed marital alliances to sustain political power. These alliances involved cousin-marriage—particularly between parallel cousins— and sibling-exchange. The strong partisanship of family alliances militated against the creation of a unified upper class. Instead, the power struggles between the Federalist and Republican families made it easier for family networks with partisan political orientations to emerge. Although the marital alliances permitted some hereditary cliques to develop, shifts in the political climate and fortunes produced a precariousness in these coalitions. Rather than facilitating the stability of the merchant class over a series of generations, the alliances made possible political alignments either within a single generation or at most extending into a second or third generation. The existence of multiple networks of intermarrying families loosened the hold of the ideas of federalism, which had been derived from the Puritan tradition. Ironically, the use of marital alliances to create political coalitions in order to maintain power eventually facilitated the downfall of the guardianship of the old families in Salem. The exodus from Salem of the major Federalist families after 1800 resulted in part from their loss of political power there.

The marital alliances created in the artisan class served a different purpose from those in the merchant class. Among the artisans, these alliances—as evidenced by the preponderance of cousin-marriages with an uncle's daughter—enhanced solidarity among male consanguineal relatives. They strengthened family bonds and enabled the apprenticeship system to remain closely tied to kinship. This high solidarity had several consequences for the politics and economy of Salem. For politics, partisanship was subordinated to family solidarity and was thus de-emphasized in the artisan class. Artisans were generally willing to go along with the political preferences of those who held the economic power of the community. For the economy, the strong ties between male relatives interfered with the requirements of free labor and rational organization in capitalism. Instead, these alliances favored the continuation of strong family government and the ideology of family guardianship.

The weakness of marital bonds in the lower class created much discontinuity in family life and made political and economic efforts in that class ineffective. The precariousness of marriage was merely another indication of the uncertainty of existence for the lower class in Salem. The lower-class family did serve a normative function in indicating to the merchants and artisans the consequences of failure to adhere to the Puritan-based family model. Matrifocality, divorce, and desertion were associated with the "lowest vices," and, by contrast, the dominant role of the male and enduring marriage in artisan and merchant families were valued as providing stability and certainty to family life. (However, in order to explain the coexistence of piety and poverty, it was necessary to introduce the concept of bad luck or unfortunate circumstances as an alternative to immorality as a basis for being poor, divorced, or deserted.) Thus, even lower-class marital instability served to protect the Puritan-based family model.

The differentiation of social classes that took place in Salem from its founding in the seventeenth century to the end of the eighteenth century affected the ability of the Puritan model of marriage and family life to maintain the social order. From the beginning, family government was considered by the Puritans as an aspect of community government, and the family was thereby tightly integrated into the political structure of Salem. As the merchant class became the dominant political force by the end of the 1700s, the factionalism and segmentation of merchant families into congeries of conjugal units created a fluidity in community power. This unsteadiness of power by coalitions of merchant families could have resulted in a reasser-

*   *   *

Family, Politics, and Marital Alliances

tion of control by the artisan class, were it not for the non-political emphasis of the alliances between artisan families. (However, it is unlikely that the strong solidarity of artisan kinship networks failed to influence the political life of the community at all. These tight-knit networks must have been able to provide blocks of Republican or Federalist votes.) In contrast, the emergence of a sizable laboring-class, whose family life was often disorganized and unstable, detracted even further from the ability of the élite to maintain political power. The threat of violence and deviant behavior was ever-present as a force opposing the moral foundations upon which the Puritan-derived community and family structure was built. Given the attributes of the families in the various social classes, the élite could no longer be effective as the guardians of virtue in Salem.

5

Family and
Socialization

This chapter explores patterns of socialization in Salem in
the 1790-1810 period in terms of (1) requirements of secular callings, (2) parental discipline, (3) the education system, and (4) the demographic base. These explorations
suggest how socialization was related to norms governing
family and community organization.

Secular Calling and Socialization

A central task for the early New England Puritan was to
create an order on earth for the glory of God. As an instrument of God, the Puritan felt an obligation to create a

*   *   *

Family and Socialization

society based on ethical control rather than on ritual obser-
vances. Since man's actions could not influence his eternal
state, his motivation for organizing such a society was to
"prove" that he was among the Elect.

According to Parsons's interpretation of Weber, "the
inner isolation, the suspicion of all things merely human
and worldly, the abhorrence of 'idolatry' turned the energy
of the Calvinist into the service of impersonal ends" (Parsons, 1949, p. 526). As secular callings, occupations were
evaluated by their usefulness to the welfare of society (and
their usefulness, in turn, was measured by the rewards they
procured). Entrepreneurship became a most pious calling
in the society. The discipline of a secular calling heightened
the value not only of avoiding unnecessary consumption
but also of using time productively. Weber suggested that
eventually a utilitarian motivation replaced religion as the
basis of attitudes toward secular calling. Ascetic devotion
to a secular calling, however, remained intact.

Weber did not concern himself with the manner by
which Puritan or post-Puritan families created men who
were driven compulsively in their callings. Still, norms consistent with this conception of secular callings governed
Puritan homes. Calhoun (1945, I, p. 112) writes:

> Of course to the stern Puritan, inexorably utilitarian, what
> afforded amusement seemed sinful. Child nature being
> depraved and wicked must be dampered. Play instincts were
> inexcusable. . . . Home discipline was relentless. Stern and
> arbitrary command compelled obedience, submissive and
> generally complete. Reverence and respect for older persons
> was seldom withheld. Adults believed in the rod as an instru-
> ment of subjugation.

The discipline preached by ministers and described in
books on etiquette was also harsh and rigorous. Children

were sometimes regarded as animals to be broken of their "brutishness" and their "self-will and stubbornness."

Yet some specialists in the history of American Puritanism indicate that "the Puritans were neither prudes nor ascetics. They knew how to laugh, and they knew how to love" (Morgan, 1966, p. 64). Given the emphasis on entrepreneurial initiative, the parents apparently realized it would be unreasonable to cow their children entirely. Children were entitled to their amusements and games. Even a strict disciplinarian like Cotton Mather indicated: "I will have my table talk facetious as well as instructive, and use much freedom of conversation in it. . . . I would never come to give a child a blow; except in case of obstinacy or some gross enormity" (Calhoun, 1945, I, p. 113).

The contradictory prescriptions in bringing up children seem to reflect the norm: whatever does not interfere with one's general or particular calling is permitted. (The general calling is, of course, God's "calling of men to salvation." The particular calling refers to the occupation by which a man earned his living.) It is true that one purpose of education was to restrain individuals "from the lewd and wild courses by which too many children are betimes resigned up to the possession of the devil" (Cotton Mather; quoted in Morgan, 1966, p. 94). Since children were believed to be born in evil, education was supposed to restore righteousness: "If we *accustom ourselves to bear the Yoke in our Youth*, it will afterwards fit more *easy* on our Necks, it will not gall and fret us" (Foxcroft, quoted in Morgan, 1966, p. 94). However, in élite families there was no reason for *complete* self-denial. This moderation makes understandable (1) the laws permitting the wealthy and other highly respected families to wear fancy clothes, and (2) the approbation of the affluent to live in elaborate houses, eat expensive food, and engage otherwise in conspicuous consumption without being accused of gross impiety. These acts, which would be considered with horror if they were performed in the artisan classes, were instead signs of success among the affluent. Hence, socialization practices were moderate in the merchant class as compared with the artisan class.

The Federal theology and the social structure derived from it served to guide the Puritans and their descendants in socializing children. First, the élite, who might be contaminated by their contact with the outside world, were exempted from having to prove their state of grace and were freed from harsh discipline. To attain high socioeconomic status meant some freedom from the ascetic life. Class differences in asceticism thus spurred many artisans toward upward social mobility. Second, by having the élite serve as a buffer against the outside world, the values of the artisan class could remain uncontaminated by secular and heretical influences, and artisan families could be readily dominated politically and economically.

Moderation in the socialization of children among the élite had had a long history in New England. Bailyn (1955, p. 109) remarks that whereas the elder John Winthrop, governor of the Massachusetts Bay Colony, was severe, dignified, stern, and introspective, his son John was the reverse: a genial, outgoing, broad-minded man. There was a comparable difference in first-generation Puritan William Pynchon and his son John; unlike his son, William was considerably polemical in spirit (Bailyn, 1955, p. 218). Other examples abound in historical literature (for instance, Morgan, 1942).

For those seventeenth-century Salemites who were not at the upper socioeconomic levels, socialization seems to have been quite severe. Penalties meted out by the General Court to the merchant-professional class were sometimes harsh, too, but these were generally remitted; the sentences were more signs of disapproval than of punishment. Besides, men of property were exempt from whipping and were given the kinds of sentences that could be easily remitted: a fine, disenfranchisement, exile. Poor men, however, faced penalties that were supposed to import severe discipline: whipping, public display on the gallows, branding. These penalties could not, because of their immediate character, be remitted; they were intended to induce firm self-discipline (Zanger, 1965). Thus, for that portion of the population whose election to grace was not apparent, the early Puritans prescribed socialization practices more severe and rigorous than it did for the recognized Elect.

The emphasis upon severity of discipline in both the seventeenth and the eighteenth centuries may be interpreted in the context of the apprenticeship system. Even in early nineteenth-century Salem, the apprenticeship system still played an important part in socialization. Citizenship was connected with strict adherence to moral precepts and with economic success; simultaneously, the chances were high that a parent might not survive to the adulthood of his children. Given these conditions, the apprenticeship system ensured a means for socializing children regardless of the survival of their parents, and it established secular callings for them. In order to operate effectively, however, the system demanded much impulse-control, self-discipline, and hard work from both masters and apprentices.

Children, regardless of their familial connections, often lived with families other than their own either as apprentices or as students. Boys were generally apprenticed to learn a trade and girls to learn housekeeping. The custom of placing children in other families had existed in England before the seventeenth century and was justified "on the grounds that a child learn better manners when he was brought up in another home than his own" (Morgan, 1966,

p. 77). The show of affection by parents was considered inimical to the creation of discipline in children. Hence, often in preadolescence the children were occupied with work and study. Here again the seventeenth-century Puritans imitated the biblical Hebrews.

The inhibition of parent-child displays of affection is consistent with the position taken by Ariès (1962) that the apprenticeship system places community relationship before family relationships. This inhibition operates to minimize the importance of the conjugal family in the socialization of children.

As late as the early 1800s, parents considered separation from children to be beneficial to socialization. In 1815, B. W. Crowninshield, then Secretary of the Navy, noted in a letter to his wife (EIHC, 1947, p. 131): *"Little Sally,* I wish it was not necessary to pack her off; altho I do not see that it will hurt her, but perhaps make her better." This sentence suggests some parental reluctance to "pack" the child off, an ambivalence not generally so apparent in artisan families. This ambivalence regarding the child's independence may have led to child-rearing techniques among the merchant class which softened precepts regarding self-reliance and self-discipline.

In the artisan class, tied closely to the apprenticeship system, the situation was different. One of the consequences of the apprenticeship system was the creation of strong bonds between males. The apprentices often formed a cohesive group in their long periods of living together and managing under the authority of their master craftsmen. Moreover, male relatives relied on one another to provide apprenticeships for their children and for jobs afterward. The strong bonds between men and the emphasis on strict discipline suggest the necessity for a norm of repression of eroticism and hostility. Normally men did not complete their apprenticeship until the age of 21 and did not marry until they were free of obligations to their master. It is to be noted also that the early American Puritans were for the most part artisans who had grown up in, and had favored, the apprenticeship system. This emphasis upon male solidarity under the apprenticeship system is consistent with patriarchal discipline in family life and with the authority of community over family in maintaining control over the young.

Parental Discipline and Socialization

What happened to socialization as Salem changed from an agrarian and fishing community to a seaport? By the Revolution, the idea of family government had declined somewhat in America. This change is noted in reports by travelers that, for example, "one of the greatest evils of a Republican form of government is a loss of . . . subordination in society . . . . Boys assume the airs of full-grown coxcombs. This is not to be wondered at, when most parents make it a principle never to check those ungovernable passions which are born with us, or to correct the growing vices of their children" (in 1807; quoted in Calhoun, II, p. 64). Calhoun also reports a decline in the harshness of parental discipline. Yet this period of diminished discipline is also the time in which Salem achieved its greatest eminence as a commercial community. Merchants rather than artisans dominated its life.

The continued presence of a highly structured, but open, class system after the Revolution implied the perpetuation of contradictory norms of child-rearing from earlier Puritan days. The child-rearing norms for the different classes had to be known throughout the community;

otherwise, they would lose their value as symbols of class membership and as motivation for social mobility. Discipline of the artisan families was considered to be good; so was the indulgence of merchant families. Asceticism of the artisan class was also considered good, but expression of the merchant class was, too. The problem was to determine whether these had been applied properly in the socialization of children.

The solution to this problem was simple: the right amount of childhood discipline and permissiveness had been applied when the probability of an individual's achievement was high. This probability was high when the person spent his time purposefully. Since the individual's destiny later in life determined whether the discipline in childhood had been appropriate, departures from child-rearing norms could be observed only *after the fact* in deviant, "unsuccessful" adults. If the deviant's parent had been a strict disciplinarian, then obviously his discipline had been *too* harsh; if the parent had been indulgent, of course he had been *too* indulgent. The norm in child-rearing was thus "moderation." Following the logic derived from Puritanism, moderation was natural, and excess unnatural.

Excessive indulgence was indeed considered evil. This vice included both self-indulgence and parental indulgence. Parents were expected to show their love—but only in moderation. This inhibition of affectional displays is consistent with the emphasis on the importance of firm "family government" in producing disciplined children, geared to upward social mobility and to status maintenance. Bentley (1909) warned "of the danger of indolence, & the want of resolution in the Parents."

However, just as excessive indulgence was considered a vice, so was extreme harshness. Severity in bringing up children was also believed to be unnatural; it, too, implied a lack of self-restraint by parents. To be excessively strict in rearing children was regarded as inhuman. Bentley comments on the role of the severity of parental discipline in a case of suicide:

> July 29, 1792—Sunday. . . . A late painful bereavement, by which the world is deprived of a very hopeful youth, may owe its cause to the excessive severity of parental discipline, & an over hasty temper. There is want of affection, but a great want of self government. These cases are recorded that I may be furnished from my own observations of the last effects of moral evils.

Giving full vent to passion and impulse was considered unnatural and could have dire consequences. Bentley provides numerous examples of the unhappiness resulting from injudicious behavior. The lesson generally learned was that the whole family suffered:

> May 12, 1790. Strange commotions in a family subject to evils, attended with great alarms. A Proof that intoxication will bring a man to make the greatest sacrifice of his peace, domestic enjoyment, & reputation. Capt. Mason contrasts a very pleasing deportment in common life with strange excentricities. His daughter was sick, for whom he is soon to provide in life. Concern arising from sympathy itself occasions gloom, brings on intoxication, which vents itself in rage, & horrid execrations. This scene is attended with horror . . .

Analyses in previous chapters indicated a strong bond in artisan families between brothers and between male relatives in general. However, since the apprenticeship system was based on authority and a sense of duty (rather than on a camaraderie), open competitiveness in work and play among male relatives was minimized, and the ideal of *machismo* did not develop. Instead, under these circumstances, the solidarity between men facilitated the repression of intrafamily aggression in order to sustain relationships in which family, work, and authority were closely interwoven.

Yet not all deviance in socialization was attributed to evil and unnatural excesses—too much severity or too much lenience—in child-rearing. Biological causation was also applied to explain the deviance of pious people. Hereditary mental illness was recognized, as indicated in Bentley's report about the Becket family:

> June 30, 1816. . . . Such a case [Hanna Rowell's] Extraordinary. Her Father W. Becket died on 1783 after having confined himself for many years to his house from hypocondria. He was a corpulent man. His wife [Mary Becket] now living at 88 years of uncommon activity, a Murray, has long been subject to periods of derangement. She is now actually of a sound mind & an intelligent & very agreeable woman. Her Eldest Son [Retire] has had his spells but is now in his shipyard. Her second son [James] has long kept house. Refuses all fire, will not leave his chamber or shift his cloathes or bed unless obliged to do it. Her third son has nothing remarkable about him. Her d[aughter] Brown has long been in derangement. . . . Lately buried a son entirely gone in madness, now a daughter, & the remaining six, to say no more, exceedingly excentric. This is the only branch in which it has gone to the third generation. . . . Her [Hanna's] husband [Thomas Rowell] from domestic vexation, has gone to Maine & has been absent nine months. Not heard of for six months.

In addition, mental illness was ascribed to "certain disorders of body & commonly fevers." Indolence and unrea-

sonableness were then exempted from interpretation as
"evil," but were considered merely circumstantial. Biological causation in mental illness, as in marital and family
problems, permitted exceptions from the ideological association of deviance and disgrace. According to Bentley:

> July 15, 1791. Examples of transient deliriums are not infre-
> quent. A Miss Barton, since Derby, was the first example &
> recovered with Kitteridge at Andover. Mr. J. Pratt recovered
> at the same place in a few months. A Mr. Tozzer has recov-
> ered after a few months. A young woman Bisby, is now at
> Andover, & a Mr. J. Chipman, a worthy merchant, is now in
> the same state. There is also a Mr. Phippen, but his disorder
> is hereditary. There was also a young Palfrey, whose delirium
> has impaired the vigour of his mind, & tho' not productive of
> idiotism, it has left an indolent habit, very different from his
> former manners. There was a Mrs. Safford, alias ____, who
> after delivery was in this state, & it was mistaken & urged on
> as a conversion, but the disorder being cured, she recovered.
> There was a young Lawyer, Pynchon, but it was accounted
> for by a very irregular life, which he has at present reformed.
> A Mrs. Frank [Rachel, wife of Joseph Frank], so called, of
> Jersey Island, has been in a continued delirium for several
> years. There have been several other examples which have
> occurred in the Charity House. All these cases have followed
> certain disorders of body & commonly fevers. They have
> been attended with considerable emaciation, & have come on
> after long complaints of weakness. The frequent use of
> evacuations & the country air have not failed to restore the
> patients, after fair experiments. They only remain subject,
> who have not made a fair experiment of the country air, such
> as poor people.

Possibly, the prevalence of mental illness may have
remained at a constant rate throughout the colonial period.
More likely, however, as Salem became a commercial cen-

ter at the end of the eighteenth century, the amount of personal stress increased. Although the norms of socialization of children in 1800 may still have been consistent with the earlier artisan economy, Salem family organization was undergoing changes more in accordance with a commercial economy. Particularly in the merchant and laboring classes, ties between conjugal families were becoming more tenuous. The Puritan family ideology persisted while the apprenticeship system was rationalized and the public school system underwent expansion. All of these events tended to increase the authority and influence of parents over children (see Ariès, 1962). Consequently, while the socialization norms continued to emphasize self-discipline, the purveyors of these norms were more often within the conjugal family. The earlier specialization, which had separated parent-child from master-apprentice roles, was lessened. This change infused the family with contradictory affectional and authority functions that likely added to stresses of parent-child interaction.

Education and the Artisan Class

The educational system in Salem during the Revolutionary era appeared to be primarily an adjunct to the apprenticeship system to socialize children in artisan families. Puritans had started schools in Salem during the seventeenth century, as shown in Bentley's (1911, III, p. 351) report:

> It is now ascertained that John Swinnerton, whose Grammar [book] has been found . . . , was a Schoolmaster. . . . John Swinnerton's Grammar is marked as his own 1652 above 30 years before he died. It will be necessary to enquire what sort of a School he kept between 1650 & 1680, because this will

determine whether private Schools were kept at this time. It
seems a writing School distinct from the Grammar School
was encouraged in 1700 & from that time a regular school
was maintained. In the preceding year, 1699, the Grammar
School had twenty Scholars.

Early in the eighteenth century, Salem established a
public school system (Putnam, 1955, pp. 24-31). In 1785,
when Reverend Bentley arrived in Salem, he found "but
one public School house, having a Grammar & Writing
School & no constant private School." By 1798, as commerce expanded, there were now "four public Schools &
three Houses, four private Schools, Women's schools for
needle work, four well known in addition to the great number for reading only." Another school was opened in 1807
"for young Negro Children in which they might be sepe-
rately instructed. In the other schools for poor children
pride will not suffer them to unite." In addition, Salem
had a special education program for young children, beginning at age five, and "for poor children to prepare them by
reading for the higher Schools." This program was maintained separately in women's schools (so called because
they were taught by women rather than men) (Putnam,
1955, pp. 52-53).

Bentley does not present information about the age
range of students. However, in describing one school he
gives the range as 5-14 years of age. This range is consistent
with age at college entry in those years, as well as with the
conception that orphaned children over 14 should have a
voice in the choice of their guardian. The age 14 thus seems
to be a transitional point in the person's life-cycle in the
Salem of 1790-1810. As for sex distribution, clearly more
boys than girls were enrolled in the public schools. There
was no segregation by sex in the women's schools. How-

ever, the grammar and writing schools separated the boys
from girls.

The curriculum varied according to the school.[1] The
public Grammar School offered a classical education, including Latin and Greek. Generally, only about 10 percent
of the male students were enrolled in the classical curriculum. The other public schools for boys focused on subjects
of a more practical nature: reading, penmanship, spelling,
grammar, and geography, in addition to some history.
Bentley notes:

> July 1, 1794. The Children read a history of the late American
> War in the style of the Scripture history, a very unsuitable
> attempt either to gain reverence to the Scriptures or knowl-
> edge of Language. . . . I must continue to blame the Book
> called the "Economy of human life" as very unfit to teach the
> English language, from the unnatural style, & oriental manner
> in which it is written.

Girls in the public schools were "chiefly instructed in
reading, from 11 to 12 o'clock & from 4 to 5 in the summer
months & longest days" (Bentley, 1911, III, p. 39). However, in the private schools the curriculum for girls was
generally broader, depending upon the school. Some of
them combined such subjects as reading with domestic
arts (like sewing). In 1807, however, plans were made to
establish a "Master's School for Misses in the fine arts for
daughters of wealthy parents." (There were also private
schools which specialized in dancing or singing.)

Instruction in the Women's Schools included hymn-sing-

[1] One private school advertised in the *Salem Gazette* (January 4, 1799) that
it offered reading, writing, arithmetic, English grammar and composition, ora-
tory, geography "with the use of the terrestrial globe," bookkeeping, surveying,
navigating, and Latin and Greek.

ing and reading. Emphasis in these schools (perhaps as well as in the more advanced schools) was upon deportment and order. As a member of the Salem school committee, Bentley observed, "All the children we saw were clean in their persons & dress & very orderly," and at another time he noted that the teacher "had above 100 boys, in good order" and that the children "for neatness & good behavior were deserving of applause." Corporal punishment of students was not abolished until 1830 (Putnam, 1955, pp. 56-61).

The emphasis on discipline and self-reliance is also implied in Bentley's note about the contrast in parental indulgence in Newburyport and Salem:

> December 9, 1798. At *Newbury Port* . . . it is observed that every person that can possibly afford it, keeps a carriage, & the children ride to & from their School. This is very different from the practice in Salem.

Enrollment and attendance in the Salem public schools was irregular. On August 29, 1803, the total male attendance at the four public schools was 213. "According to the master's books, this may be about a third of the whole number of males which is instructed in their Schools. The females may also amount to about half, & probably are three hundred" (Bentley, 1911, III, p. 39). The attendance figures for this date were normal. Male student attendance, which tended to be lower during the cold winter months, for the ensuing years was as follows:

1804	228
1805	228
1806	238
1807	290
1808	350

* * *

Family and Socialization

The increase during the last two years can be attributed, at least in part, to the opening of the school for black children. However, compared with a potential male school population of at least 1,000, attendance was very low. The proportion of children who actually attended the Women's Schools was also low; for example, 182 in 1808 (with an enrollment figure of 260). In the winter, the number dwindled. In his entry for February 27, 1809, Bentley noted, "This day we visited the Women's Schools for small & poor children. . . . The plea for the small number present was from the severity of winter & the poverty of the times which pressed upon the people."

Male children who attended the Salem public schools in the 1790-1810 period were mainly from middle-class, artisan families. Sons in poor, laboring-class families generally left school early to enter the working force. Death records contain numerous entries of 10-15-year-old boys (from poor families) who died at sea. Bentley (1907, II, p. 459) bemoaned, "Tho' the instruction be gratis, few are prevailed upon to attend." He attributed this low attendance in part to "the early employment of the children of mariners" (Bentley, 1907, II, p. 96).

Sons in wealthy families ordinarily went to private schools, which could provide adequate preparation for the university. In 1807, there were two schools "maintained by private Gentlemen with high salaries for classical education." Another was added by 1809. The 75 students "from select families" accommodated in these private schools contrast sharply with the mere 10-20 students enrolled in the public school classical curriculum. By sending their children to private schools, the parents could retain greater control over them than was possible in the public school, since the master was dependent on their good will in order to retain their children in his school.

* * *

Guardians of Virtue

With children from laboring-class families excluded by economic necessity and with children from merchant families concentrated in private schools, the public schools were left mainly to the sons of artisan-class parents. The educational system was similar in a variety of ways to the apprenticeship system: (1) through sex segregation, it served primarily males; (2) the focus of the curriculum was on practical rather than classical education; (3) like master artisans, the teachers were men and—significantly—were given the title of Master; and (4) the schools, from the Women's Schools on, placed some responsibility for instilling discipline in the hands of an outsider.

However, there were also significant differences between the educational and apprenticeship systems. Ariès (1962) suggests that the development of a school system oriented toward occupational training permitted the retention of parental authority, since the schoolmaster, unlike the master in charge of an apprentice, did not provide a home and sustenance for his students. Instead, the schoolmaster's tenure and his control over his students remained directly or indirectly (through a school board) at the pleasure of the parents. This development is consistent with the trend noted by Ariès of the simultaneous development of secular education and the conjugal unit as a family form. Both represented a decline of the control by extrafamily agencies over the socialization of children.

Socialization in Salem and its Demographic Base

The apprenticeship system seems to thrive where there is a shortage of qualified craftsmen in a protected market. During the colonial period in New England, skilled labor was in short supply (Morgan, 1966, pp. 124-125). Demographically, this situation may emerge (1) where there is a high death rate among young adults seeking to become masters in their crafts, and (2) where there are many debilitating conditions which might prevent some graduating apprentices from practicing their skills. Such a situation would permit a master to employ a large number of children and youths at minimal cost, but would preclude the emergence of significant competition which might depress the market price of finished products and services.

The uncertainties of lifespan, health, and child-raising seem to have engendered a precariousness and tentativeness of perspective. These uncertainties must have produced tremors in the religious foundations of Puritan Salem. As commerce developed, the sea became an additional source of risk to life. Although the relationship between demographic characteristics and socialization practices must be inferred indirectly in the analysis, the vital statistics, insofar as they are reliable, do provide a firm basis for interpretation. Particularly, the data on death seem to reveal the conditions under which people lived out their existence. Age at death, cause of death, differential chances of dying early for men and women, and place of death all seem significant. They indicate the kinds of risks that people faced and suggest ways in which the family was organized to meet the contingencies of the death of its members.

In terms of family relationships, a high rate of death and debilitation among young adults with minor children would imply a large number of young widows and widowers, who would then have to rely upon their elders for support or for household assistance until remarriage could occur. Accordingly, the older people in the community, who had survived the vicissitudes of youth and were living off a protected market for their goods and services, would generally have much authority and power in the family and community.

In terms of personal relationships, the high rates of death and debilitation among young adults would require everyone to develop strong moral obligations to (1) fulfill the functions of guardianship, (2) train for a secular calling, and (3) care for dependent persons. At the same time this prevalence of morbidity and mortality would force awareness of the fragility of life and the futility of deep emotional ties between persons. Young children ought not to become too attached to their parents, and vice versa. On the other hand, strong bonds between siblings and other collateral relatives were necessary for securing a good home and family government for one's children. These socialization requirements seem to have been met in the traditional apprenticeship system, which was closely tied to family relationships. The data suggest not only the demographic influences which sustained the apprenticeship system but also the events which precipitated the eventual decline of this system.

Age and Cause of Death

The data regarding the conditions under which people died in Salem are presented below. The information used in the analysis of age and cause of death was taken from the East Church lists compiled by The Reverend William Bentley from January, 1785, to December, 1819. In all, 1231 deaths are recorded.[2] In all instances, the age of the decedent is given and, except for 28 cases, the cause of death is described.

[2] In addition, there were three persons for whom Bentley did not list their sex and one case of a death reported overseas where the man was later found to be still alive.

* * *

Family and Socialization

The cause of death listed by Bentley varies in reliability. In some instances Bentley was precise, particularly in describing fevers and acute illnesses such as tetanus, cholera, West India flux, measles, or scarlet fever. In other instances, particularly for persons in a debilitated condition, the cause of death was speculative (e.g., old age, long infirmity, lethargy, or worn out). In cases of suicide, venereal disease, or death from "intemperance," Bentley delicately ignored the cause of death in his entry; these were recorded in his diary or in *Salem Vital Records*. However, because Bentley was generally meticulous in his reporting, his list is probably more reliable than others for age and cause of death.

Data on Death

Information relative to the ages of persons dying and to the cause of death will be discussed in this section. First, age-specific death rates for Salem in 1799 will be compared with those in later years, 1826-1835, to indicate the direction of change in population structure over the years. Second, the general age and sex distribution of decedents in 1785-1819 will be described. Then, more specific material will be introduced regarding differential causes of death for men and women. Finally, some implications of these data for socialization will be drawn.

Table 5-1 presents estimates of age-specific deathrates for Salem in 1799 and for Salem and New Haven combined in 1826-1835. Because of some arbitrary assumptions made in the computations, these estimates should be regarded as suggestive rather than highly reliable. The annual average of the Salem and New Haven rates for 1826-1835 is based on an analysis by Jaffe and Lourie (1942, p. 369). Unfortunately, they did not include data for children under 5 years of age or persons 80 or over. Hence, age-specific

*   *   *

rates for the 45-or-over category are not comparable for 1799 and 1826-1835. Moreover, the Jaffe and Lourie data had to be recomputed, and interpolations were made for the age-categories used in the 1800 U.S. Census report. Similar interpolations had to be made for the 1799 death data from the *Salem Gazette*. Given these cautionary remarks, the following comparisons can be drawn:

1. In the youthful age-categories, 10-25 years of age, age-specific deathrates for the two time-periods are similar. No significant change in the life-style of the young (if sex is ignored) seems to have occurred.

2. For adults, aged 26 or over, age-specific deathrates decreased appreciably from 1799 to 1826-1835. In the 26-44 category alone, the rate dropped by 5 per 1,000, from 18.5 to 13.5. For mature adults, the style of life in Salem apparently changed sufficiently to affect demographic processes. The significance of this shift in age-specific deathrates will be explored in the following paragraphs in terms of sex differences and causes of death.

The general distribution of age at death, by sex, for Salem residents in the 1785-1819 period (in Bentley's list) is presented in Table 5-2. Roughly 30 percent of all deaths occurred before the age of 6, and another 5-8 percent between the ages of 6 and 15. Before the age of 16 the proportions of males and females dying are generally similar. However, for young adults sex differences in dying become appreciable, with the percentage of men dying in this age-category almost double that for women. About one-half of the male decedents (47 percent) died between the ages of 16 and 50, as compared with only 34 percent of the women. Finally, over 30 percent of the female decedents expired after the age of 50, while only 17 percent of the men did so. These differences in the proportions of deaths, by age, of men and women are consistent with the varia-

* * *

Family and Socialization

Table 5-1
Estimated Age-Specific Death Rates for Salem in 1799 and for Salem
and New Haven Combined in 1826-1835*

Age Categories	Per 1,000 in Salem (1799)	Per 1,000 in Salem and New Haven (Annual Average 1826-1835)
Under 10 years	34.8	—
10-15	4.7	3.7
16-25	7.8	8.2
26-44	18.5	13.5
45 or over	50.1	30.6

*Rates for Salem in 1799 computed from Bills of Mortality data in *Salem Gazette* for January 1, 1800 and U.S. Census for 1800, p. 8. Rates for Salem and New Haven adapted from Jaffe and Lourie (1942), p. 369. Recomputations and interpolations were necessary to accommodate age-categories of 1800 census. Jaffe and Lourie did not include data on death for persons under 5 or for persons 80 or over.

tions in sex ratio at different age-levels in Table 4-4.

The high proportion of men dying between the ages of 16 and 30 in Salem during the period 1785-1819 seems to have provided a demographic basis for sustaining the apprenticeship system. The age distribution of deathrates suggests the following periods in the life-cycle of individuals in Salem: (1) young childhood, age 5 or under; (2) youth, roughly ages 6-15; (3) young adulthood, ages 16-30; (4) mature adulthood, ages 31-50; and finally, (5) the elderly, who would constitute the population aged 51 or over. The ages given to represent the boundaries of the life-cycle stages are, of course, rough approximations. The distribution of deaths suggests that young adulthood was a period

* * *

Table 5-2
Deaths From All Causes for Salem Residents in 1785-1819
(by age and sex)

Age (in years)	Men		Women	
	N	%	N	%
71 or over	46	6.8	94	17.1
51-70	72	10.6	79	14.3
31-50	136	20.0	104	18.9
16-30	181	26.6	81	14.7
6-15	30	4.4	41	7.4
5 or under	215	31.6	152	27.6
Total	680	100.0	551	100.0

of high risk for Salem males. This would be the time in life in which most young artisans would be establishing themselves as journeymen and masters in their secular calling.

The cause of death of young adults is of particular concern with regard to both the apprenticeship system and family life. When persons die following an accident or a brief illness, their deaths produce a sudden cessation of normal routines. However, when death occurs after a long debilitating condition, very likely the persons have been incapable of carrying out normal domestic or economic duties in their daily lives for quite some time. Other persons would then have to help support them or to undertake their domestic tasks. For adult women, roughly twice as many died following a long debilitating illness or condition as those who died after a brief acute ailment. Whereas 85 women, aged 16 or over, died of a fever or other acute ailment, 192 suffered a long-term debilitating condition prior to death.

The comparison in deaths for men and women following a chronic debilitating condition is shown in Table 5-3. For persons 15 or under, sex differences in the percentage dying from such conditions were minimal; roughly one-fourth of the males and females were involved. For children with a debilitating condition, the cause of death was ordinarily atrophy, death at birth or shortly afterwards, or feebleness, resulting in death within a few hours following birth. There were a few cases of consumption or tumors. (There were also several persons with hydrocephaly, but this condition is classified under the central nervous system disorder rather than general debilitating conditions.)

For men, there was an increasing tendency for death to occur from chronic debilitation with a rise in age. Among the younger men, consumption was the primary long-term cause of death; with increasing age other causes predominated, such as senile atrophy, decay, or old age.

For the women, a majority of the adults died from a long-term debilitating condition. Until the age of 50, consumption was by far the predominant cause of death.[3] Afterwards, certain kinds of debilitation associated with old age increased. Eighty-three of the 180 total deaths for women aged 16-50 were ascribed to consumption or scrofula. This number contrasts sharply with only four deaths ascribed to puerperal or childbed fever. Perhaps a large percentage of the women who might have been likely candidates for childbed fever had been weeded out by contracting a disease early in life; roughly half of those 15 or under had apparently died of communicable disease.

[3] Even as late as 1900-1904 tuberculosis was the leading cause of death for both males and females in the United States (Dublin, Lotka, and Spiegelman, 1949, pp. 160-161.)

Table 5-3
Deaths Deriving from Long-Term Debilitating Conditions for Men
and Women Residents of Salem, 1785-1819
(by age)

Age (in years)	Men			Women		
	Deaths from Debilitating Conditions		Total Deaths*	Deaths from Debilitating Conditions		Total Deaths*
	N	%		N	%	
51 or over	48	42.9	112	90	52.9	170
31-50	38	28.4	134	55	54.5	101
16-30	22	12.6	175	47	59.5	79
15 or under	66	27.4	241	50	26.2	191

*Of known cause; total unknown cause: 28.

Presumably there was also a large number of women
described as consumptive who survived the 1785-1819 era.
The large proportion of women who were apparently in
chronic poor health suggests that Salem women had to rely
to a considerable extent upon neighbors and relatives to
carry out their household duties. Under these conditions,
children could not expect their ailing mothers to provide
much protectiveness and devotion. Rather, the children
would be encouraged to become self-sufficient, and the
apprenticeship system constituted an institutionalized way
of inculcating this self-sufficiency.

The necessity for relying upon friends and relatives was
created not only by chronic ailments but also by absence.
With the development of Salem as a seaport in the late
eighteenth century, a large percentage of its young male

* * *

Family and Socialization

Table 5-4
Place of Death of Male Residents of Salem, 1785-1819
(by age)*

Age (in years)	1785-1800					1801-1819				
	Abroad		U.S.			Abroad		U.S.		
	N	%	N	%	Σ	N	%	N	%	Σ
51 or over	2	4.3	44	95.7	46	1	1.4	71	98.6	72
31-50	25	44.6	31	55.4	56	21	26.3	59	73.7	80
16-30	69	67.0	34	33.0	103	40	51.3	38	48.7	78
15 or under	5	4.9	97	95.1	102	1	0.7	142	99.3	143

*List of East Church, recorded by Bentley.

population spent months or even years away from home on
sea voyages. It was not unusual for a ship to be out of port
for a year or two. Thus, many of the young men left their
families in the care of relatives while they roamed the world.

The long sea voyages took a heavy toll of lives. Table
5-4 presents data on the place of death of male residents in
the years 1785-1819. Because of the decline of Salem as a
seaport in the early nineteenth century, the table presents
information regarding deaths for the period 1785-1800 and
1801-1819 separately. After 1800 ships increased in size,
and shipping suffered through embargoes and blockades.
Still, for both time-periods, a majority of the men who died
between the ages of 16 and 30 were overseas at the time. In
addition, for the 1785-1800 period, almost half of the men
who died between the ages of 31 and 50 were also overseas.
The drop in the number of deaths from the 1785-1800 era
to the 1801-1819 period can be attributed primarily to the
decrease in overseas deaths. Even some of the persons aged

16-30 who died in the United States did so upon their return home from a long voyage. Thus the prosperity of Salem and the stability of its social structure were obtained at the cost of the lives of young adult men.

Table 5-5
Deaths Deriving from Acute Illnesses (Such as Fevers, Communicable Diseases, Dysentery) and Accidents (Such as Lost or Drowned at Sea) for Male Residents of Salem, 1785-1819
(by age)

| Age (in years) | 1785-1800 | | | | | 1801-1819 | | | | |
| | Fevers, etc. | | Accidents | | | Fevers, etc. | | Accidents | | |
	N	%	N	%	Σ*	N	%	N	%	Σ*
51 or over	5	11.1	2	4.4	45	13	19.4	5	7.8	67
31-50	25	45.4	13	23.6	55	29	36.7	9	11.4	79
16-30	60	61.2	27	27.6	98	26	33.8	24	31.2	77
15 or under	47	48.0	5	5.1	98	74	51.7	3	2.1	143

*Of known causes; cause unknown 18 cases.

The risk of going to sea involved not so much the danger of being shipwrecked or lost at sea as the contraction of exotic diseases. Table 5-5 compares the percentage of deaths derived from such illnesses as fever and those attributed to accidents such as loss or drowning at sea. For the 1785-1800 era, the probability of a man 16-30 years of age dying from a fever or acute communicable disease was more than twice that of dying from an accident, yet both tended to occur overseas. By the 1801-1819 period, however, the probabilities of death by fever and by accident were roughly equal for this age-range. For mature

adult men (ages 31-50) the probabilities of dying either of
fever or by accident declined from 1785-1800 to 1801-
1819. Obviously fewer mature men were at sea.

To summarize, the data on the deaths of young men
and women (especially ages 16-30) indicate that the demographic base in Salem was such that young adults were
often unable to carry out their family duties without the
assistance of relatives and friends. Many young women
were in a chronic state of disability, and the men were
overseas. The much-needed assistance was provided by
older relatives, particularly widowed grandmothers. This
situation was especially prevalent among lower-class
families.

Various consequences of maternal disability and paternal absence for the Salem seaman's family are suggested in
letters written over a two-year period by a woman to her
husband on a long voyage (EIHC, 1958, pp. 151-155):

December 24, 1828. . . . i went down to mothers the night
that you went to sea for i could not bear to see the house
after It lost its chief attracion. . . .

July 18, 1829: I set down to inform you that the first
day of this month you had A Son. i cant say a grate Boy but
thare is room a nuf to grow. . . . I am very Week indeed and
have been this four months but hope With the blesing of
god i shall soon gett my health and Stregth. . . . it appears
to me if you every Live to get home I shall bee happy But i
am afraed that your Boy will say father first. . . .

May 16, 1830: . . . I embrace the happy oppertunity of
imfirming you of My health wich has not been very good since
you left Salem. . . . when i think that you are again to bee
gone a nother year I can hardly bear the thought. . . . I have
moved in Mr. Swasyes house close by Mothers as i have been
from thar over a year and it is plesinter to bee near your
friends. Eliza Bedny has lost both her children and Carealine

184

Guardians of Virtue

has lost her little Boy. likewise your Aunt Bedny is dead.
your folks is all well and send there love to you.

May 23, 1830: . . . my health . . . is i thank god better
than it was. . . . Accept the sincere love of your Absent Wife
and Son who will bee erly taught to love his absent Father.

November 28, 1830: . . . I now imbrace the oppertunity
of imforming you of my Health wich is a great deal better
than it was the last time i wrote. . . . I supose you would like
to hear from your boy. he is well and A runing round the
room while i am a wrighting. he begins to say some ____
and already nows whear his Dear Father is that is your
protrait. . . . he will bee Large enuf to go down on the Wharf
with you iff this teduoius voage ever comes to a end.

The dissipation of paternal authority in the lower segments of Salem society, while the ideal form remained
patriarchal, is evident in the above letters. Various letters
show the close relationship existing between the writer,
Mrs. Nichols, and her mother and sister. For example,
"Margaret [the sister] says she has kissed the boy a hundred
Times for you" or "Mother and Margaret . . . think thear
never was such a child before. . . . Mother says you must
not forget her present. she expect you will bee so proud
of him that you will think he is worth a great deal more."
Mrs. Nichols, however, makes no mention of male relatives
in her letters to her husband. Female relatives seem to
dominate the child's life.

The special significance attached to the mother-child
relationship among Salemites is also suggested in the following letter from Mary Low to her husband Seth (EIHC,
1955, p. 256):

I believe you will be very much amused with Charles. He is
a queer child, though sometimes a noisy one. He does not
talk much better than when you left. He brought home a

* * *

Family and Socialization

> little boy with him the other day by the name of Archer. I
> asked the boy if he had any mother. Charles [aged 4] says:
> "Yet[h], and ever so many fathers!"

However, probably more than anything else, the letters
by Mrs. Nichols convey the loneliness and uncertainty of
life in Salem families of low socioeconomic status. Bulletins
on her chronic ill health, interspersed with news of the
death of close relatives—children as well as adults—even
while she dotes on her child, provide the focus of her letters.
Her communications to her husband suggest a precarious
situation in which her anxieties and fears drive her toward
close family ties. (Mrs. Nichols died about a year after
writing these letters.)

Becoming a seaman on eighteenth-century sailing-ships
also entailed much risk that one might contract a fever and
die abroad. It was then a matter of chance that one would
return at all, and those who survived beyond their seagoing
days could well regard themselves as being predestined for
Election (even if they were not Calvinists). Survival probably suggested to them a charmed destiny.

In the passage of time from 1785 to 1819, profound
changes seemed to be occurring in Salem. The decline of
shipping meant that previous shortages of journeymen and
masters no longer existed. There was greater competition
for jobs in marketing and manufacturing; the situation was
no longer conducive to the traditional apprenticeship system. Moreover, in the late eighteenth century, when many
men died overseas, the wealthier elders at home were able
to sustain a strong position in politics. Those who died
overseas were generally poorer and were not members of
the élite. However, with the decline of shipping, the death
rate of lower-class men decreased. The survival of the poor
had political, as well as familial, consequences.

The entire system of enterprise (including shipping) was well suited to the Federalist conception of society. But the waning of the shipping industry permitted poor men to exert greater political influence in Salem. As they survived in greater numbers, Salem shifted politically from Federalist to Republican dominance at the beginning of the nineteenth century. Thus, the Derby family declined, the Federalist élite began to migrate to Boston, and the Crowninshields and other Republicans from the East End of Salem took over.

The rise of Republicanism, as opposed to Federalism, in the early years of the republic, had more than political significance. Republicanism was associated with the French Revolution by the Federalist writers, and it signified the value of the equality of mankind. For the Federalists, Republicanism was a symbol of mob rule and Godlessness. Godlessness implied that the Republicans lacked ethics; they were the embodiment of evil, and were against the traditional Puritan ideals of family government and firm discipline.

Yet, while the economic and political institutions of Salem seem to have been affected by the decline of Salem as a seaport at the beginning of the nineteenth century, there is no indication that family norms and values as such changed appreciably. If anything, the young men, being at home rather than overseas, tended to strengthen their roles in their families. Accordingly, responsibility for the socialization of children, instead of falling to kin because of chronic maternal disability or of the fathers' absence at sea, could remain within the conjugal family.

Conclusion: Individual Risk and Familial Certainty

Federalist theory prescribed the establishment of a hierarchical order, as opposed to chaotic relationships, in all facets of community life. As the basis for the social struc-

* * *

Family and Socialization

ture, the family had the responsibility for the maintenance of this order and consequently for instilling self-discipline and self-control in all individuals. Yet notions of piety and divine order, which were part of federalist theology, connote more than the mere repression of hostility. They also involve the controlled expression of love, loyalty, and duty. There were thus conflicting aims in socialization in the family organization derived from Puritanism: repression of antisocial impulses and the expression of pious sentiments.

The ambivalence between imposing discipline and permitting self-expression was resolved in the Salem family by a norm of moderation. In the expression of sentiment, moderation implied strong personal ties while at the same time introducing mechanisms to maintain some social distance even within the family. Hence children were sent away to be raised by relatives at times, and even those with wealthy parents often served long apprenticeships. With regard to discipline, moderation implied neither an excess of parental indulgence nor too severe an upbringing.

Since moderation assumes that neither extreme laxity nor harshness is appropriate in the administration of discipline, no objective criteria exist to indicate when the boundaries of moderation have been crossed. Parents themselves must decide when they are deviating from accepted norms. They may be more willing to err on the side of being either (1) too strict in their discipline and too restrained in their show of sentiment, or (2) too lenient in discipline and too effusive in their display of sentiment. The merchant and laboring classes tended to err on the side of effusiveness and the artisan class on the side of restraint.

In the conflict between risk-taking and family security, the merchant families and artisan families took different courses. For the merchant class, the emphasis was upon risk-taking, whereas the artisan class stressed family security and conformity. With the relatively large amount of property at their disposal, merchants could take considerably more risks than could artisans. Still, to minimize their risks, the merchants (as noted in Chapter 3) formed family partnerships to pool their capital. The skilled craftsmen, however, could not risk the laxity of discipline found in merchant families. The artisan class required family connections to procure valuable apprenticeships, and this situation led to the use of sons and nephews as apprentices and to the creation of first-cousin marriages with the masters' daughters. The strong reliance upon family bonds in the artisan class seemed to demand an emphasis upon order, authority, and duty in the family. Here the need for discipline and self-control in personal development was especially desirable.

In this chapter, the relationship between socioeconomic status and socialization was shown in several ways. First, the public schools used an apprenticeship model in their organization. The curriculum was practical; order and discipline were emphasized, the authority of the schoolmaster was generally unquestioned, and sex segregation was practiced. These characteristics resembled the structure of artisan families. Yet the fact that the schoolchild remained under the aegis of his parents added to the strength of conjugal-family relationships and to the parents' influence in socialization. Second, the demographic base affected family relationships differentially by socioeconomic level. The high deathrates among adults and the prevalence of chronic disability made it necessary to rely upon one's relatives as a form of insurance. Relatives could provide guardianship and apprenticeships for the young and were generally a source of economic and personal aid. From the viewpoint of the economic system, the high deathrate among young men reduced competition and, in this manner, sustained the apprenticeship-artisan arrangement. A large working force of unbound labor failed to develop as long as the deathrate for young men was high.

The high deathrate among young adults (as well as the ubiquity of chronic disability) supported the values of the maintenance of authority and of duty toward relatives. The emphasis on these values was stronger in the stable artisan class, which relied more on human resources, than in the merchant class, which could fall back upon property. Since the laboring class had neither the stable human resources nor the property to sustain its stability, the lower-class family was not so severely constrained in the maintenance of its authority and in devotion to family obligations.

The high deathrate and the threat of poverty most likely reinforced conceptions of fatalism. In the Puritanism of the seventeenth century, the Calvinist doctrine provided the basis for ascribing causation to fate. Toward the end of the eighteenth century, bereft of these religious underpinnings, fate assumed a different interpretation. In a community where epidemics sometimes raged, where contraction of a disease overseas was common, where the ravages of tuberculosis were evident everywhere, and where illness could well reduce a family to poverty, healthy and wealthy adults could well conceive of themselves as leading charmed lives. Although by 1800 they could no longer claim predestined eternal grace, the rich merchants and master craftsmen could regard themselves as chosen by fate for a secular state of grace. Through them, the Puritan compulsion toward the continual accumulation of wealth survived in Salem in a transfigured way at least to the end of the eighteenth century.

There seems to be a close connection between Federalism, fatalism, and the threat of death and poverty. As the deathrates of adults declined in Salem after 1800, so did the Federalist conception of society. The Federalist con-

*   *   *

Guardians of Virtue

ception, based on fate, sustained the apprenticeship system and the dominance of the merchant-professional élite. As members of the laboring class began to survive to later maturity in larger numbers, the community relied less on family authority, duty, and hierarchical order to maintain the social structure. In politics, the Federalist party lost out; the Republicans took over. Yet the familial, educational, political, and religious ideologies established under Federalism survived to affect the socialization of succeeding generations.

6

Conclusion: Family and Community Structure

This study of Salem families around the year 1800 suggests the process by which Puritan doctrine eventually stimulated economic growth and modernization in an ethnically homogeneous community. The preceding analyses indicated ways in which family organization throughout the social order complemented the development of commercial enterprise. With the writings of Max Weber and Philippe Ariès as background, this chapter discusses the results of the analyses. While the findings are most relevant for helping us to understand the process of modernization, they also provide a context for observing the perseverance of earlier cultural models in contemporary society and for examining the emergence of new family patterns.

* * *

Guardians of Virtue

Weber and Ariès

Max Weber was interested in religion as a triggering mechanism which set off events ultimately shaping modern economic and political institutions. Although there were conflicting statements in Calvinist writings, Weber suggested that the influence of Protestantism lay in the congruence of its essential elements with the spirit of rational capitalism. His major interest was to demonstrate the motivational force of Calvinist Protestantism. Given this intention, Weber did not concern himself with ephemeral economic and political conditions involving technological change, war, revolution, or depression. Since Weber did not empirically examine the process by which Calvinistic norms became functionally autonomous, he may have misinterpreted the nature of Protestant influence on capitalism.

Weber's position that Puritan theology promoted the development of modern capitalism has been challenged by some historians. To Philippe Ariès, for example, religious ideology is peripheral in forwarding the evolution of modern social structure. Instead, Ariès emphasizes demographic and technological factors in his explanation of change. Taken together, however, the perspectives of Weber and Ariès may shed new light on an old problem in social causation.

The data on Salem show that by the Revolutionary era each social class, with its characteristic family form, provided its own unique contribution to a growing commercial spirit. Thus, the commercial spirit may be seen to emerge, not as the ideological property of a single social class, which is what Weber implies, but rather as an evolving consensus: an intermeshing of separate social classes

having descended from the earlier federated community,
which in turn had originated in Puritan theology.

The Puritan-Based Family Model

Around 1800, when Salem was at the height of its brief
success as a seaport, it still held vestiges of Puritan family
and kinship organization, modeled after the Old Testament
patriarchal structure. The Puritan conception of the ancient
Hebrew family embodied permissibility of first-cousin marriage, partible inheritance (with a double portion to the
eldest son), solidarity between male relatives, and a convic-
tion that conformity to the traditional norms of family life
would enable the community to prosper.

With belief in a connection between family government
and prosperity as the ideological core for both the Hebrew
code and the Puritan ethic, it is understandable that the
concept of family government came to be extended to the
community. The Puritan community was regarded as
analogous to the Hebrew tribe, with the "visible saints" as
the "chosen people." Left unchecked, the American Puritans developed a federated community organization (Haskins 1960, pp. 141-162). Legitimized by "federal theology,"
community federation existed on two levels: (1) family
government, which, through the parents, supervised conduct within the household unit, and (2) town government,
which, through its overseers, supervised the conduct of
family units. By dominating town government, the Puritan
élite had privileges and power denied to families and individuals whose predestined state of grace was doubtful. This
federated structure persisted long after the Puritan religious
basis for community organization had died away.

It is Ariès's approach which captures those forces at

work undermining relationships upon which the federated
life-style was based. Ariès attributes the movement away
from medievalism to the decrease in death rates of children,
to the decline of apprenticeships as socializing agencies, and
to the growth of occupationally oriented educational institutions. As Salem social structure became more highly differentiated with the passage of time, it manifested the
changes in deathrates, apprenticeships, and schools which
Ariès associates with modernization. By the end of the
eighteenth century, diverse family forms could be identified in the three major social classes: the merchant class,
the artisan class, and the laboring class. The following sections discuss the relationship of family organization within
each class to the economic and political life of Salem
around 1800.

The Merchant Class

In the merchant class, the role of the patriarch as entrepreneur was emphasized. The merchant patriarchs sent out
ships on long voyages, which sometimes took two or three
years to complete. In the course of a single voyage, several
ocean crossings at various parts of the world might take
place. Ships loaded in Sumatra might unload in the Middle
East or the Mediterranean before taking up another Far
Eastern cargo for the voyage home. These long voyages
pulled men away from their families and exposed them to
a variety of exotic life-styles. The merchants made extensive use of unskilled and unbound labor, such as mariners
and shoremen and introduced a highly rational organization
in the division of labor in their shipping and commercial
enterprises.

Since the patriarch-entrepreneurs took many risks in
order to earn high profits, they had to find ways to minimize them. One way that they could minimize risks was to

* * *

Conclusion: Family and Community Structure

hire relatives whom they could trust. In families like the Crowninshields or the Derbys, sons, nephews, or the children of close friends often acted as sea captains or supercargoes or were given other positions of trust such as correspondents in distant lands. A second way was to pool capital in family partnerships, which apparently also symbolized a high degree of family solidarity. Third, they extended their sources of capital and trusted personnel by creating family alliances through marriage.

Certain characteristics of family life were more effective than others in fostering entrepreneurship. First of all, patriarchal authority helped to develop an effective division of labor in commercial enterprises. Second, partition of inheritance forced heirs to pool their resources, thereby encouraging family unity (at least symbolically). Third, first-cousin marriage and sibling-exchange facilitated the creation of alliances and partnerships in business and politics. Fourth, the designation of the eldest son as the primary heir or successor to the family headship (symbolized by the double portion of inheritance prior to the Revolution) facilitated the stability of the commercial enterprises past a single generation. Fifth, the creation of family alliances signified a strong emphasis upon kinship solidarity, which could then be translated into trust and expansion of the sources of investment capital.

While family organization in the merchant class was generally effective in fostering collective entrepreneurship, it produced other results as well. First, decisions in business sometimes caused merchants to question the competence and integrity of relatives (who were also their partners). Consequently, suspicion and distrust eroded family partnerships, which had been originally intended to symbolize solidarity. Second, coalitions between families were used not only for commercial endeavors but also for the formation of political factions. These factions tended to become separate social worlds, each with its own set of business arrangements and of intermarriages among first cousins and among sets of siblings. The formation of these factions split the community politically and socially, but still facilitated political control by the merchants and professionals over the artisans and laborers. The artisan who did not conform to deference-voting patterns found himself blacklisted in all firms associated with a particular faction (cf. Thernstrom, 1964). Furthermore, the factionalism of the merchant-professional class implies a conception of society as a highly unstable, competitive arena. The factions themselves were competitive enterprises which extended into almost all facets of family and community life and conflicted with the conception of an orderly federated community.

The dominance and life-style of the merchant-professional families rested on their success in shipping and commerce. The shipping industry in turn had a powerful influence on the entire social structure of Salem, an influence which was felt not only in its division of labor but also because of its demographic effects. Because of the high rate of fatalities from exotic diseases, there was a continual shortage of young men in Salem. This shortage made Salem a convenient locus of migration. Outsiders could not compete with the local artisans but did provide a reservoir of unskilled labor. In contrast, those persons who survived to become successful artisans and merchants had a long life expectancy, during which time they could continue to accumulate wealth and power for themselves and their heirs.

In brief, involvement in business enterprise brought power to merchant-class families, but it also created a divisiveness among them despite the gains that were made by pooling resources and by creating alliances. For the most part, these alliances were ephemeral; although ties with the extended family might not be completely broken (so that resources could again be pooled), conjugal families tended to be autonomous.

The Artisan Class

The role played by artisan-class families in the development of business enterprise was different from that of the merchant class. The artisans' industry was still largely home-based but provided an arena for socializing children particularly suited to the pursuit of business enterprise.

As formulated by Max Weber, the needs of rational capitalism for the maximization of profit included (1) the presence of a pool of unbound labor and (2) the separation of household affairs from work. In both of these areas, the artisans restrained the progress of rational enterprise. Their economy, with its apprenticeship system, relied heavily upon bound labor. By collaborating with the merchant class on numerous issues, the artisans were able to mount enough power to keep down the numbers of unbound, skilled labor. As for the relationship between family and work, the artisans' households held apprentices as members, and noneconomic factors influenced interaction between master and apprentice. In taking on apprentices, artisans frequently favored relatives over others who might be more capable and efficient. All of these actions often ran counter to the emphasis on maximization of profit among artisans.

While the artisan family as an economic institution may have deviated from the norms of rational capitalism, the artisan family as a socializing agency did not. Even in early colonial days the artisan class supported greater conformity to the Puritan codes of conduct, while the merchants championed a more liberal position (Bailyn, 1955). The patriarch-artisans acted as guardians of Puritan-derived norms and values and tried to instill discipline and self-control in the young. Precisely because of their situation in which they controlled much cheap labor through apprenticeships, the patriarch-artisans were in a position to extol the virtues of hard work and to denounce the evil of indolence. They could justify these prescriptions not through base financial motives but by showing that the success of the unproven apprentice-relative was dependent upon internalizing such values. (As an analog, professors today exhort their graduate students to work hard as research assistants on the basis that the knowledge gained will enable the students to become masters of their academic field; the successful undertaking of the professor's research is only incidental.)

Findings relevant to the maintenance of artisan-class families and the apprenticeship system include the following: (1) the relative longevity of parents and the large number of children in need of apprenticeships, (2) the strong ties between male kin as suggested by the tendency toward first-cousin marriage with a blood-uncle's daughter, (3) the strong role of family symbolic property, such as a highly skilled occupation, which was then transmitted from one generation to the next among relatives, (4) the expectation that relatives would assist one another both in time of need and to ward off need, and (5) the tendency of individual members of the family to remain in the same general locale as their close relatives.

The above findings suggest that strong, stable extended-family relationships persisted in the artisan class long after the merchant families had fragmented themselves into numerous conjugal units. With extensive periods of apprenticeship and with emphasis on occupation as a family property, the young had little autonomy in their daily lives. The establishment of a public school system permitted the artisans' children to remain in their families of orientation

Conclusion: Family and Community Structure

longer. Yet, as the children grew older, they still faced an
apprenticeship of several years. With children trained by
relatives outside the conjugal family, extended families
formed tight social networks, and the conjugal family did
not achieve complete independence as a social unit.

Despite their dependence on relatives, the artisan families, rather than the more independent merchant families,
inculcated in children the drive and skills needed for
upward social mobility. This tendency calls into question
the assumption by many sociologists that the small, isolated
conjugal-family form is more appropriate than the close-
knit extended family in fostering social mobility in industrial society. Sennett (1969) found a similar relationship
between extended-family households and social mobility
in Chicago during the period 1870-1890.

The Laboring Class

The families making up the laboring class tended to
deviate markedly from the norms upheld by the merchant
and artisan classes. The laboring class was made up mainly
of "strangers" to the community, outsiders to the body
politic. It was not until the first decade of the nineteenth
century that members of this class were accorded voting
privileges. In the previous decades, they had even been
warned out of town. This group, which contributed the
day labor to the economy, constituted a marginal category
of the population. The rationalization of the division of
labor toward the end of the eighteenth century required
just such a malleable population segment to meet the needs
of the moment.

The undefined family organization of the laboring class
allowed its members to become victims of circumstance.
While the patriarch-dominated artisan class generally
resisted encroachments on its skills and its domestic base,

the loose mode of family organization in the laboring class
left each member open to exploitation regardless of age or
sex. Because of their lack of conformity, members were
sometimes placed under the guardianship of the town
overseers or were sent to the charity house. School attendance was low, and special-education programs failed to
solve the problems of inadequate preparation in a school
system which was geared to the needs of artisans families.
In addition, the fragility of marital ties precluded the development of patriarchal authority; men in the laboring class
died early, and widows generally remarried (and probably
dominated) other lower-class men. In general, the lack of
organized authority in the laboring-class families seems to
have complemented the power of élite families in commercial enterprise and community organization.

The strong role of the community in the guardianship
of children from laboring-class families must have interfered with the organization of the households as autonomous conjugal units. The participation by community
authorities in decisions affecting the lives of family members among the poor and deviant blended family life and
community life so that distinctions between them were
easily lost. (Even today the easy access of social workers
and other community representatives into the families of
the poor and deviant may inhibit the development of
strong family boundaries and may instead contribute to
the disintegration of family units.) Moreover, since the age
of family members in the laboring class meant little in the
differentiation of occupational or familial roles, the lower-
class family probably failed to develop a concept of
parental guardianship to prepare children for adult life.
Factors inhibiting the development of stable conjugal
units made the poor and the deviant easy targets for
exploitation.

201

* * *

Conclusion: Family and Community Structure

Class and Capitalism

The configuration of family life in the merchant, artisan, and laboring classes gave to Salem commercial enterprise its peculiar characteristics. The intense competition within the merchant class required the pooling of family resources and the creation of family alliances to embark on commercial ventures with some sense of security. Unintentionally, artisan families were responsible for the socialization of persons who were motivated in the extreme to strive for upward social mobility. The artisan class emphasized the instrumentality of family and kinship toward the achievement of security in livelihood and security in status. Finally, the frequently female-dominated family of the lower class allowed the further separation of domicile and economy which the development of commercial endeavor demanded. The loosely organized lower-class family made possible a pool of geographically mobile, unbound labor. Later studies of industralization in New England show that migrants and the old laboring class constituted the factory labor force; the artisans continued at their trades for some time, until the need for their skills finally died out (Thernstrom, 1964).

In general, the findings of this investigation provide some support for Max Weber's contention that in the final analysis the Puritan ethic promoted the development of capitalistic enterprise in America. The differences in findings can be ascribed mainly to methods of analysis.

Weber's discussion of the ideal-type entrepreneur placed the ascetic, responding to his calling, at the very center of the Protestant ethic. He regarded firm dedication to acquisitiveness as an expression of worldly asceticism. Strong family ties would interfere with the cultivation of industriousness inherent in the calling and with the reinvestment of profits to make more profits. In short, Weber saw the family solely as an agency for consumption hindering the development of rational capitalism.

In *The Protestant Ethic and the Spirit of Capitalism*, Weber considered post-Revolutionary Massachusetts to be the archetype of the Protestant ethic in action. Yet in Salem at the height of its phenomenal success as a seaport, families were organized in ways which did not oppose capitalistic enterprise. In fact, the one successful merchant who most conformed to Weber's ideal typical entrepreneur was despised by the community for his subordination of family and friends to acquisitiveness. Contrary to Weber's position, the family functioned as an instrument rather than an obstacle in the development of rational capitalism.

It is ironic that the asceticism which Weber considered crucial to the spirit of capitalism was less characteristic of entrepreneurs than craftsmen, whose family ties were strongest. Weber himself (1958, p. 65) points out that Benjamin Franklin's printing business was essentially a handicraft enterprise and that

> it was by no means the capitalistic entrepreneurs of the commercial aristocracy, who were either the sole or the predominant bearers of the attitude we have here called the spirit of capitalism. It was much more the rising strata of the lower industrial middle classes.

The role of the family thus seems to be central in the transition of Salem from a community with strong medieval overtones to a commercial town. Were it not for the Puritan heritage, the kinds of family organization in the various parts of the social structure would have been different. Were it not for the demographic and technological changes, the federated community structure might have persisted. Hence, Salem at the end of the eighteenth cen-

tury represents an historic moment when the families as a
group were able to marshall their material and ideological
resources in ways which changed the shape of their society
dramatically.

The Post-Revolutionary American Family

Ideas about the family derived from Puritanism and based
on biblical injunctions were diffused throughout the United
States after 1800. Emigration to the West is apparent in
many of the Salem genealogies. New England seaports
became obsolete as large sailing vessels and steamships were
built, and prosperous merchants migrated with their families to such commercial centers as New York and Philadelphia. Artisans and unskilled workers traveled southward
and westward as well. Partly as a consequence of the
decline of these seaports, the Puritan version of the biblical-
based family model spread and influenced states outside of
New England. Early Illinois marriage law was typical in the
following Levitical norms. According to a footnote in the
1856 edition of *Illinois Statutes of a General Nature*
(p. 739), "under the statute of 1819, males of the age of
seventeen and females of fourteen, could be joined in marriage, 'if not prohibited by the laws of God.' 'A.' married
the daughter of his sister, and the marriage was held to be
within the Levitical degrees, and voidable, though not
absolutely void." In other states, such as the Michigan
statutes of 1857 (Vol. II, p. 950), marital proscriptions also
adhered to the Levitical code, although no mention was
made of a biblical reference.

The contemporary American family still bears some
resemblence to its ancestor in Salem of 1790-1810. The
similarity is apparent in the norms of family government,

many ideas about marriage, and some socialization practices.

With regard to family government, studies of juvenile delinquency, mental illness, and other forms of deviance lay the blame on the family for the failure of its members to develop into responsible citizens in the community. The ideal of domestic control still dominates the thinking of many political leaders and educators. There appears to be a general consensus that the poor and their children are incompetent to manage their affairs; social workers, counselors, and other agents of welfare institutions are then brought in to assist them.

The biblical kinship structure upon which the Puritans modeled their family relationships has persisted in a modified form in modern society. Its close association with middle-class society even today is indicated in relationships among kin. Biblical kinship is characterized in part by the symbolic incorporation of a man or woman into his spouse's family of orientation. In eighteenth-century Salem, a man might use the terms "brother" and "brother-in-law" interchangeably in referring to his wife's sibling. Similarly, he might refer to his wife's mother as his "mother."

The perseverance of biblical kinship in contemporary middle-class families is suggested by the contrast in kinship terminology used to address in-laws in middle and lower socioeconomic groups. A study of kinship in a midwestern community indicates that middle-class young adults address their in-laws as "Mother" and "Father" when they feel close to them but address them by their first names when they feel more distant. The reverse is true for low socioeconomic classes, with the first name used to indicate a close tie. This usage of kin terms of address implies that a middle-class adult (regardless of motivation) acknowledges a status which he acquires in his spouse's family of orientation. This status is equivalent to that of his spouse and defines

*   *   *

Conclusion: Family and Community Structure

the married couple's relationship to their in-laws. For the lower class, however, kinship ties formed with affines represent merely formal relationships, whereas the *real* ties of married couples with in-laws are personal. As personal ties, the relationships with in-laws do not depend so much upon norms that govern status as on ways people relate to their in-laws as individuals. Hence, for the lower class, marital ties are not the gateway to a symbolic incorporation into one's spouse's family of orientation. Rather, as in the old Salem lower class, marital ties are relatively weak and bonds with maternal kin are frequently strong (Farber, 1971).

As in other aspects of family life, there appears to be some carryover of the Puritan-based model in areas of the socialization of children. In upper-class socialization, there is apparently emphasis upon moderation in child rearing; there is generally no attempt or "need" to inculcate strong motives of upward social mobility. For the middle classes, however, achievement motivation seems to be strong. This class focuses upon delayed gratification patterns, the suppression of eroticism which might interfere with achievement, and the recognition that effective authority (rather than a laissez-faire parent-child relationship) should exist. By contrast, lower class socialization places little emphasis upon delayed gratification, repression of eroticism, and the development of effective authority patterns; instead, lower-class families are plagued by many authority problems. Thus the general patterns in the socioeconomic variations of the Salem family seem to have persisted into modern urban society (Kohn, 1969; Farber, 1971).

To the extent that norms governing the contemporary family resemble those pertaining to the Salem family of the period 1790-1810, the American kinship system can be said to retain the norms and values of the Puritan-based family as a cultural model.

Change in the Family

Despite some resemblences between the contemporary family and the family of 1800, obvious changes have occurred. There has been a decline in patriarchal control, a greater isolation of conjugal families from relatives, an increase in divorce, a rise in juvenile delinquency, and an increased participation of women in the labor force. These chances have often been described as "family disorganization," "family problems," and "decay of the family."

The application of these descriptions to trends in family life implies that the basic cultural model has remained the same but that the conformity of actual behavior to ideal norms and values has declined. Some sociologists attribute this discrepancy to "strain" which results as the family vies unsuccessfully with other institutions to retain its traditional functions (Parsons and Bales 1955; Firth 1964, p. 66).

Many observers have explained the departure from conduct appropriate to the traditional cultural models of the family as resulting from major social crises. For example, the crisis of rapid urbanization uproots many people and forces them to apply their existing norms and values—for they are committed to no other—in a markedly different environment. Similarly, in modern society, wartime is associated with departures from routinized ways of doing things. Total mobilization of society to wage war necessitates changes in actual behavior but not in ideal family models. Women work in defense plants and young men interrupt their careers to enter the military forces. Many dislocations in family life connected with "moral decay" occur—couples enter hasty marriages, there is much promis-

* * *

Conclusion: Family and Community Structure

cuity, families move away from their relatives, and wives are left alone at home while their husbands are gone for months or even years. Thus in World War I and later in World War II, there were many deviations in behavior from the traditional cultural models.

World War II especially produced many modifications in family life. Labor shortages drew women, racial and ethnic minorities, the elderly, the young, and other marginal workers into industry. The concentration of war industries in urban centers generated housing shortages and revised living standards. As important, urban institutional arrangements—police, local government, entertainment, schools—were unprepared for the surge of demands for services. Consequently, the assimilation of marginal workers and rural migrants into the usual institutional life of metropolitan communities was hampered. The overburdening of urban facilities placed much strain on family relationships (Wirth, 1943, p. 71).

Yet, while wars may weaken commitments to traditional cultural models, they generally do not produce ideologies which embody new family models. Rather, wars are seen as temporary dislocations by forces outside the society. On the other hand, economic depressions more often stimulate the production of such new models by signaling to many people that something is wrong with the society; they provide the impetus for making a sharp break with the past.

During depressions the male workers are especially hard hit. In the early 1930s industries in which male workers were concentrated were more seriously affected than those relying on women workers (Stouffer and Lazarsfeld, 1937, pp. 28-35). In that decade, paternal prestige and authority frequently declined, particularly when fathers were unemployed. This shift was usually profound in families where mothers or children became the primary breadwinners. In the depth of the Depression, children of unemployed fathers tended to be more critical of them than were children of working fathers, more so in families where the mothers were also highly critical of them. The Depression also brought a decrease in marriage and birth rates as well as an increase in illegitimacy. It did produce a few strengthening effects; there was less divorce, and children stayed in school longer. But by far, the major influences were negative.

As anyone would expect, deviation in family behavior from norms associated with the traditional cultural models tends to occur among the young. Age was also a factor in unemployment during the 1930s. Young, inexperienced workers faced the most difficulties in finding employment (Stouffer and Lazarsfeld, 1937, pp. 35-36). Their disenchantment with the established way of life resembled that of the black youth of the 1960s. This disenchantment stimulated them to seek radically different cultural models.

Deviation from tradition during the Depression of the 1930s was in many ways more extensive than that in wartime since both young and established families alike were greatly affected: the economic and social stability of the older generation was gone. Hence, more people began to seek new ways to organize and to justify their existence.

Newer family models, emerging since the 1930s, emphasize companionship and affection rather than asceticism and self-discipline in organizing family relationships (Burgess, Locke, and Thomes, 1963: Miller and Swanson, 1958). They have their roots in conceptions of the role of the family associated with the welfare state, equalitarianism and cultural pluralism, and the personal freedom afforded by modern urban society. The diffusion of the newer family models was furthered by the enactment of govern-

* * *

Conclusion: Family and Community Structure

ment programs in the 1930s to permit security in retirement and in time of personal crisis. Many of the reforms
had been initially proposed in early socialist political plat-
forms. As efforts to reduce the financial burdens of families, these reforms lessened the necessity and thereby
lowered the motivation, to accumulate personal savings
and investments. As the general population accepted these
reforms minus their ideological implications, it also
accepted the family models which they presupposed.

By the 1960s, the increase in the bureaucratization of
society and the lessening of control over one's own destiny
further alienated many young people from the traditional
cultural models of family life—including those generated in
the 1930s depression. The powerlessness fostered by this
large-scale bureaucratization engendered both withdrawal
from participation in traditional institutions and attempts
to revise them radically. This reaction to the power of
bureaucracies—especially government—to act as guardians
of virtue has focused public attention upon the inequities
in American society. The result has been strong demonstra-
tions against war, against the systematic discrimination of
minority groups in education, industry, and politics, and
against the entrenched older generation's reluctance to
sincerely try to solve the major social and economic problems of modern society. The emerging generation regards
many leaders as guardians of evil.

Because family and kinship organization is an integral
part of social structure, the alienated critics of modern
society have tended to reject the forms of family life tradi-
tionally associated with it. These forms, they recognize, are
intimately tied to the same political and economic systems
which gave rise to the impersonality of overpowering
bureaucracies and to the social injustices present in society.
Instead of setting forth discipline and hard work as virtues

that families should foster, the dissident critics of contemporary family life have offered humanness, sharing, and love. Instead of strictness in child raising, they have emphasized romanticism, with each individual expressing himself in his own way. In breaking with the past, the critics have drawn upon radical family models, often devoid of their sectarian, ideological underpinnings, for developing new family and household arrangements. They are the new guardians of virtue.

Conclusion: Fluctuations or Long-Range Trends?

Social scientists differ in opinion with regard to whether recent trends in family life actually represent a shift in basic values. Some, like Talcott Parsons (1955), see the trend of the future American family as an elaboration of the Puritan-based model adapted to urbanized, industrialized society. Others, like Seymour Lipset (1961, pp. 246-252), conceive of change as cyclical, with equalitarian norms dominant at one time and élitist norms prevailing at another.

The position here is that crises in American society, dramatized by the Depression of the 1930s, have crystallized and diffused cultural models which evolved during the past century. These models imply certain socialization practices, consumption patterns, and life organization, which are contrary to the traditional accumulation of personal wealth and achievement in occupation. To be sure, wealth and power are still, to a considerable extent, concentrated among families of "the rich and the super-rich" (Lundberg, 1968). Insofar as new cultural models gain a foothold with the replacement of generations, however, the present legitimation of that power and wealth may

* * *

disappear. Since the family is still the central arena for the socialization of children, consumption of economic goods, and maintenance of highly personal relationships, the family models of the emerging generation may stimulate change in the economic, political, and educational institutions in the United States. The lesson of Salem of 1800 may be relevant; the recent emergence of experimental family models may well indicate the future of American society.

One of the shortcomings of social science is that while long-range secular trends, as opposed to short cycles, must by definition persist from one generation to the next, the lifespan of the social scientist is obviously restricted to a single generation and the timespan of his data is often even briefer. There is, therefore, considerable uncertainty as to whether the changes in the models of social life which he postulates are actually occurring. Moreover, gaps in historical data raise the question of whether they ever existed.

References

Anonymous
1848 *The Aristocracy of Boston: Who They Are, and What They Were: Being a History of the Business and Business Men of Boston, for the Last Forty Years.* Boston: Published by the Author (By one who knows them).

Arìes, Philippe
1962 *Centuries of Childhood: A Social History of Family Life.* New York: Alfred A. Knopf, Inc.

Atkins, Gaius G., and Frederick L. Fagley
1942 *History of American Congregationalism.* Boston and Chicago: Pilgrim Press.

Bailyn, Bernard
1955 *The New England Merchants in the Seventeenth Century.* Cambridge: Harvard University Press.

1960 *Education in the Forming of American Society.* Chapel Hill: University of North Carolina Press.

Bardis, P. D.
1964 "Family Forms and Variations Historically Considered." In *Handbook of Marriage and the Family*, ed. Harold T. Christensen, pp. 403-461. Chicago: Rand McNally & Co.

Batchelor, G.
1948 "The Salem of Hawthorne's Time." Essex Institute Historical Collections 84:72-74. (Originally a lecture given in Salem in 1887 and published in the *Salem Gazette*, March 11 and 18, 1887.)

*   *   *

References

Belknap, Henry Wyckoff
    1927   *Artists and Craftsmen of Essex County, Massachu-setts.* Salem, Mass.: The Essex Institute.
    1935   "Simon Forrester of Salem and his Descendants." Essex Institute Historical Collections 71:17-59.

Bentley, William
    1905-   *The Diary of William Bentley.* Salem, Mass.: The
    1914   Essex Institute. (Four volumes)

Burgess, Ernest W., Harvey J. Locke, and Mary M. Thomes
    1963   *The Family: from Institution to Companionship.* New York: American Book Company.

Calhoun, Arthur W.
    1945   *A Social History of the American Family.* 3 vols. New York: Barnes and Noble. (Published originally in 1917.)

Demos, John
    1965   "Notes on Life in Plymouth Colony." *William and Mary Quarterly* 22:264-286.
    1970   *A Little Commonwealth, Family Life in Plymouth Colony.* New York: Oxford University Press.

Dublin, Louis I., Alfred J. Lotka, and Mortimer Spiegelman
    1949   *Length of Life: a Study of the Life Table.* Rev. ed. New York: Ronald Press.

(EIHC) Essex Institute Historical Collections
    1859-   Essex Institute Historical Collections. Salem, Mass.:
    1969   The Essex Institute. (Volumes 1-101)

Erikson, Kai T.
    1966   *Wayward Puritans.* New York: John Wiley & Sons.

Falk, Ze'ev
    1964   *Hebrew Law in Biblical Times.* Jerusalem: Wahrmann Books.

Farber, Bernard
    1964   *Family: Organization and Interaction.* San Francisco: Chandler Publishing Company.

1968 *Comparative Kinship Systems: A Method of Analysis.* New York: John Wiley & Sons.

1969 "Marriage Law, Kinship Paradigms, and Family Stability." In *Transactions of the Second International Seminar* (Rennes, April 10-13th, 1969), ed. Clio Presvelou and Pierre de Bie. Louvain, Belgium: International Scientific Commission on the Family.

1971 *Kinship and Class: A Midwestern Study.* New York: Basic Books.

Firth, Raymond
1964 "Family and Kinship in Industrial Society." *The Sociological Review:* Monograph No. 8, pp. 65-87.

Fowler, S. P.
1860 "Records of Overseers of the Poor of the Old Town of Danvers, for the Years 1767 and 1768, by the Chairman of the Board, Capt. Elisha Flint, with Notes." Essex Institute Historical Collections 2:85-92.

Fuess, C. M.
1956 "Essex County Metamorphosis." Essex Institute Historical Collections 92:4-17.

Gerth, Hans, and C. Wright Mills
1946 *From Max Weber: Essays in Sociology.* New York: Oxford University Press.

Greven, P.
1966 "Family Structure in Seventeenth-Century Andover, Massachusetts." *William and Mary Quarterly* 23:234-256.

Habakkuk, H. J.
1955 "Family Structure and Economic Change in Nineteenth Century Europe." *The Journal of Economic History* 15:1-12.

Haskins, George Lee
1960 *Law and Authority in Early Massachusetts.* New York: Macmillan Company.

*   *   *

References

Hehr, Milton G.

1964a   "Theatrical Life in Salem, 1783-1823." Essex Institute Historical Collections 100:3-37.

1964b   "Concert Life in Salem, 1783-1823." Essex Institute Historical Collections 100:98-138.

Indovina, Frank J., and John E. Dalton

1945 &   *Statutes of All States and Territories with Annota-*

1956   *tions on Marriage, Annulment, Divorce (with Cumulative Supplement).* Santa Monica, Calif.: Law Publishing Company.

Jaffe, A. J., and W. I. Lourie, Jr.

1942   "An Abridged Life Table for the White Population of the United States in 1830." *Human Biology* 14:352-371.

Keezer, Frank H.

1923   *A Treatise on the Law of Marriage and Divorce.* Indianapolis: Bobbs-Merrill Company, Inc.

Keim, Clarence R.

1926   *Influence of Primogeniture and Entail in the Development of Virginia.* Ph.D. dissertation, University of Chicago.

Kohn, Melvin

1969   *Class and Conformity.* Homewood, Ill.: Dorsey Press, Inc.

Kunstadter, P.

1963   "A Survey of the Consanguine or Matrifocal Family." *American Anthropologist* 65:56-66.

Lamb, Robert K.

1952   "The Entrepreneur and the Community." In *Men in Business,* ed. William Miller, pp. 91-119. Cambridge: Harvard University Press.

Leavitt, W.

1861-   "History of the Essex Lodge of Freemasons." Essex

1862   Institute Historical Collections 3:37-47; 84-94; 121-132; 174-185; 207-218; 253-271 and 4:255-262.

Lehman, Frederick K.
1963   *The Structure of Chin Society.* Urbana: University of
            Illinois Press.

Lévi-Strauss, Claude
1969   *The Elementary Structures of Kinship.* Boston:
            Beacon Press.

Lipset, S. M.
1961   "Equality and Achievement in American Life." In
            Issues of the Sixties, ed. Leonard Freedman and
            Cornelius P. Cotter, pp. 246-252. Belmont, Calif.:
            Wadsworth Publishing Company.

Lundberg, Ferdinand
1968   *The Rich and the Super-Rich.* New York: Lyle Stuart.

Main, Jackson Turner
1965   *The Social Structure of Revolutionary America.*
            Princeton: Princeton University Press.

Marx, Karl
1964   *Early Writings,* trans. and ed. T. B. Bottomore. New
            York: McGraw-Hill.

Miller, Daniel R., and Guy E. Swanson
1958   *The Changing American Parent.* New York: John Wiley
            & Sons.

Miller, Perry
1949   *The New England Mind: The Seventeenth Century.*
            Boston: Beacon Press.

Morgan, Edmund S.
1942   "A Boston Heiress and her Husbands." Publications of
            the Colonial Society of Massachusetts 34:499-513.

1966   *The Puritan Family.* New York: Harper. (Earlier edi-
            tion published in 1944).

Morison, Samuel Eliot
1941   *The Maritime History of Massachusetts 1783-1860.*
            Boston: Houghton Mifflin.

Morris, Richard B.
1927   "Primogeniture and Entailed Estates in America."
            Columbia Law Review 27:24-51.

1930   *Studies in the History of American Law.* New York: Columbia University Press.

Parsons, Talcott
1949   *The Structure of Social Action.* Second ed. New York: Free Press.

Parsons, Talcott, and R. F. Bales
1955   *Family, Socialization and Interaction Process.* New York: Free Press.

Perley, Sidney
1924-   *The History of Salem, Massachusetts.* Salem, Mass.:
1928   Sidney Perley. (Volumes 1-3)

Perry, Ralph B.
1944   *Puritanism and Democracy.* New York: Vanguard Press.

Phillips, J. D.
1937   *Salem in the Eighteenth Century.* Boston: Houghton Mifflin.

1944   "Salem Merchants and Their Vessels." Essex Institute Historical Collections 80:261-270.

1947   "Who Owned the Salem Vessels in 1810?" Essex Institute Historical Collections 83:1-13.

Powell, Sumner Chilton
1963   *Puritan Village.* Middletown, Conn.: Wesleyan University Press.

Putnam, E.
1921   "Note on the Population of Salem, 1637." Essex Institute Historical Collections 57:149-150.

Putnam, Perley
1955   "Extracts from the Salem School Records." Essex Institute Historical Collections 91:24-74. (Written originally in 1834.)

Queen, Stuart, and Robert W. Habenstein
1967   *The Family in Various Cultures.* Philadelphia: J. B. Lippincott Company.

Rantoul, R. S.
1897   "The First Cotton Mill in America." Essex Institute
        Historical Collections 33:1-43.

Ropes, B.
1955   "Autobiography." Essex Institute Historical Collec-
        tions 91:105-127.

Salem Gazette
Passim   January 12, 1790-December 31, 1810.

Salem Vital Records
1916-   *Salem Vital Records to 1840.* Salem, Mass.: Essex
1925   Institute. (Volumes 1-6)

Samuelsson, Kurt
1961   *Religion and Economic Action.* Toronto: Heinemann.
        (Published initially in 1957)

Saveth, E. N.
1963   "The American Patrician Class: A Field for Research."
        American Quarterly 15:235-252.

Scheftelowitz, Erwin Elchanan
ca. 1948   *The Jewish Law of Family and Inheritance and Its
            Application in Palestine.* Tel Aviv: Martin Feucht-
            wanger.

Schneider, Louis
1970   *Sociological Approach to Religion.* New York: John
        Wiley & Sons.

Scoville, Warren C.
1960   *The Persecution of Huguenots and French Economic
        Development, 1680-1720.* Berkeley and Los Angeles:
        University of California Press.

Sennett, Richard
1969   "Middle Class Families and Urban Violence: The
        Experience of a Chicago Community in the Nine-
        teenth Century." In *Nineteenth Century Cities:
        Essays in the New Urban History,* ed. Stephen Thern-
        strom and Richard Sennett. New Haven: Yale Univer-
        sity Press.

* * *

References

Silsbee, N.
1899   "Biographical Notes." Essex Institute Historical Col-
            lections 35:1-79. (Written 1836-1850)

Stouffer, Samuel A. and Paul F. Lazarsfeld
1937   "Research Memorandum on the Family in the
            Depression." New York: Social Science Research
            Council (Bulletin 29).

Thernstrom, Stephan
1964   *Poverty and Progress: Social Mobility in a Nineteenth
            Century City.* Cambridge: Harvard University Press.

Towner, L. W.
1966   "The Indentures of Boston's Poor Apprentices: 1734-
            1805." Publications of the Colonial Society of Massa-
            chusetts 43:417-468.

U.S. Census
1791   Return of the Whole Number of Persons Within the
            Several Districts of the United States, According to
            "An Act Providing for the Enumeration of the Inhabi-
            tants of the United States," passed March the first,
            one thousand seven hundred and ninety-one. Phila-
            delphia: Childs and Swaine: 24.

1801   Return of the Whole Number of Persons Within the
            Several Districts of the United States, According to
            "An Act Providing for the Second Census or Enu-
            meration of the Inhabitants of the United States."
            Washington, D.C.

Walzer, Michael
1965   *The Revolution of the Saints.* Cambridge: Harvard
            University Press.

Waters, T. F.
1897   "The Early Homes of the Puritans." Essex Institute
            Historical Collections 33:45-79.

Weber, Max
1958   *The Protestant Ethic and the Spirit of Capitalism.*
            New York: Charles Scribner's & Sons. (Published
            initially in 1904-1905.)

1963   *The Sociology of Religion.* Boston: Beacon Press.

Whitney, W. T.

1958   "The Crowninshields of Salem: 1800-1808: A Study
                 in the Politics of Commercial Growth." Essex Insti-
                 tute Historical Collections 94:1-36 and 79-118.

Wirth, Louis

1943   "The Urban Community." In *American Society in
                 Wartime,* ed. William F. Ogburn, pp. 63-81. Chicago:
                 University of Chicago Press.

Zanger, Jules

1965   "Crime and Punishment in Early Massachusetts."
                 William and Mary Quarterly 22:471-477.

Index

Index

Index

Index